M.L
REA

FRIENDS OF ACPL

232 H26i
HEIM, S. MARK.
IS CHRIST THE ONLY WAY?

2265714

**DO NOT REMOVE
CARDS FROM POCKET**

ALLEN COUNTY PUBLIC LIBRARY

FORT WAYNE, INDIANA 46802

You may return this book to any agency, branch,
or bookmobile of the Allen County Public Library.

DEMCO

Is Christ the Only Way?

Christian Faith in a Pluralistic World

S. MARK HEIM

Judson Press ® Valley Forge

Allen County Public Library
Ft. Wayne, Indiana

IS CHRIST THE ONLY WAY?

Copyright © 1985
Judson Press, Valley Forge, PA 19482-0851
All rights reserved. No part of this publication may be reproduced, stored in a retrieval system, or transmitted in any form or by any means, electronic, mechanical, photocopying, recording, or otherwise, without the prior permission of the copyright owner, except for brief quotations included in a review of the book.

Unless otherwise indicated, Bible quotations in this volume are from the Revised Standard Version of the Bible copyrighted 1946, 1952 © 1971, 1973 by the Division of Christian Education of the National Council of the Churches of Christ in the U.S.A., and used by permission.

Other quotations of the Bible are from *The New English Bible*. Copyright © The Delegates of the Oxford University Press and The Syndics of the Cambridge University Press 1961, 1970.

Additional quotations are from the HOLY BIBLE New International Version, copyright © 1978, New York International Bible Society. Used by permission.

Library of Congress Cataloging in Publication Data

Heim, S. Mark.
  Is Christ the only way?

  Bibliography: p.
  Includes index.
  1. Jesus Christ—Person and offices. 2. Christianity and other religions. I. Title.
BT202.H42 1985   232   84-27767
ISBN 0-8170-1027-0

The name JUDSON PRESS is registered as a trademark in the U.S. Patent Office.
Printed in the U.S.A.

Contents

Introduction	7
Part I: Presuppositions	11
1. Out of the Question?	13
2. Red Herrings	33
3. Jesus in Particular	51
Part II: According to the Scriptures	67
4. The One in God's Place	69
5. The One in Our Place	83
6. One Whose Place Cannot Be Taken	95
Part III: Christ and Other Ways	109
7. Live Options	111
8. Is Christ the Only Way?	129
Suggestions for Further Reading	151
Notes	153
Index	157

Introduction

Is Christ the only way? An example is probably close at hand. A neighbor's son comes home from college in Ohio with his girl friend, a Hindu premedical student from India. Not far outside your town in rural New Hampshire a farm has been made over into a community for followers of an Eastern guru. In many American cities the sinuous gold of a minaret rises around the corner from white colonial steeples.

No matter what part of the Western world we live in, we are likely to encounter faiths professing other names than that of Jesus Christ. When we do, what are we to make of Scripture's assertion that there is no other name under heaven by which persons may be saved? Approximately one-third of the world's population is Christian. What is Christ's relationship to the other two-thirds?

Over the past two hundred years Western Christians have written one of the most significant chapters of world history, an achievement often unrecognized because of its extension over time and its dogged dailiness. This is the missionary story. Its impact, whether reverenced or despised, is huge. Without doubt, the mainspring of that movement was a passionate conviction that the people of the world were perishing for the lack of knowing Christ. Do Christians still share that conviction? Should they?

Much has been written about the forces which have made this missionary conviction problematic for many Christians. For one thing, our perception of our own culture has shifted. We see the faults of our culture and the sins of the Christian church. We have learned to acknowledge that the supremacy of Christ is not logically implied by the material success of the Christian West, nor by any supposed moral superiority of Christians to other people.

Just as important has been a growing distrust of exclusive claims of any sort. The terrible experiences of two world wars and the awareness of economic and racial injustice have shaped a suspicion about any belief that might become an ideology of superiority. Thus, people seriously doubt that it is safe or sound to believe that *anyone* has *the* truth.

The question is not just whether we ought to proclaim Christ. If we believe Christ is *our* Lord, we would be expected to do no less. The question is whether it is objectively *true* that Jesus Christ is the way, the truth, and the life. It is not just a matter of whether we ought to preach Christ, but of whether people ought to believe us. Is Christ the only way, the definitive truth, the abundant life?

Such absolute language may be out of fashion in some circles. It may pain those of us who have learned to love not only other cultures, but the virtues and wisdom of other faiths. It may appear arrogant. Yet none of these feelings is quite to the point. Either there is one way (however rich and complex it may be), or there are many ways, or there is no way. That is the extent of the possibilities.

I am ready to argue that the Christian church is correct in regarding Jesus Christ as final and decisive. The crucial question is, "Decisive in which way?" As Christians we ought not to compromise the affirmation that "Jesus is Lord." Yet, on the other hand, we must be vigilant not to import into this affirmation anything that has to do only with our particular religious rules, our institutional channels, or our relative cultures. We must not muffle Christ's claim on the world, but we must beware of being excessively jealous for Jesus.

If the Christ we profess is the Christ revealed in the New Testament, we must be guided by his attitude, his distinctive blend of the presumptuous and the humble. If we are to carry forward the claims of such a Lord, we must follow in these unique footsteps.

This book approaches our topic in three parts. First I deal with what might be called presuppositions. Even among Christians today, discussions of this topic often end before they begin. We are acquainted with courtroom procedures where cases are decided before the evidence is even presented, because of legal technicalities or principles. A similar verdict is often rendered on the universal Christ. Such presuppositions are so widespread that we must consider them first.

The second part of the book is intended to clarify what Christians should and do profess of Christ. If Scripture is our guide, how are we obligated to affirm Christ as the one true way? In what respects is the Christian faith exclusive and in what respects is it not?

In the third section we return to the question "How are Christians to understand Christ in a pluralistic world?" I will survey the range of answers which Christians today are giving to this question, answers which are debated in theological terms by professors and church leaders but are expressed just as often and forcefully in plain talk by Christians within our own communities or congregations. These views differ in their estimate of other faiths, the importance of evangelism, and the nature of salvation. Consideration of these options will lead me to a statement of some of my own conclusions.

This is not a book *about* other faiths, or the relationship between Christianity and any specific religion or ideology. It is about the way in which Christians should deal with the *fact* of pluralism in our modern world. One of the most important questions for Christians today is not only what we think of other faiths, but how we understand our *own* faith, for this perception will certainly shape all of our relationships. Therefore I have devoted significant space to the scriptural basis of our claims, on the assumption that when facing a difficult problem, it always helps to read the directions.

I have also tried to keep the book itself largely free of reference to other writers or long quotations. Footnotes will indicate where in fact I am dealing with the views of prominent thinkers, but I have attempted to keep the focus on the *substance* of various views or arguments, as opposed to names or labels.

It is my hope that this book will serve to stimulate discussion. Nothing is more important for us today than to come to a secure understanding of our own faith in relation to all the other religions which swirl around us. Uncertainty about our own central conviction will not serve either religious cooperation or sound evangelism. Those who confess Christ with clarity of heart and mind will practice both.

I owe thanks to many people for their assistance in the preparation of this book. I am grateful to my colleagues at Andover Newton Theological School, Gabriel Fackre and Max Stackhouse, for the use of their published and unpublished material. The participants in the 1984 international seminar at Mansfield College, Oxford, contributed much to my thinking and tested an early version of portions of the book. I also benefited immeasurably from being privileged to attend the Sixth Assembly of the World Council of Churches at Vancouver, British Columbia. In that "town meeting" of the world church I learned much of other cultures and other faiths.

Above all, I would like to thank Melissa Lewis Heim for her insight and suggestions. For both of us, I acknowledge Sarah and Jacob for all they have taught us of "pluralism" in many forms!

S. Mark Heim

Newton, Massachusetts
June, 1984

PART I

Presuppositions

PART I

Presuppositions

Out of the Question?

From time to time in newspapers or on television there is news of the Flat Earth Society, a group of persons who continue to insist that the earth is flat. On one television program a member of the society was presented a photograph of the earth taken from a space capsule. Shaking his head appreciatively, the man said, "Isn't that something? From space it actually *appears* as though the earth were round." Of course, he went on, there must be some explanation for this illusion, since the earth is in fact flat.

We all have convictions that go almost that deep. If a usually dependable friend is late for an appointment, we do not immediately suspect that she has maliciously stood us up. The problem must be a traffic jam or some emergency. We operate with certain principles which do not so much answer our questions as indicate what kind of answers will *count* at all.

A famous historian has called such principles "absolute presuppositions." If, without advance warning, we happen to see a lunar eclipse on a summer night, we do not tell ourselves "the moon is perhaps being eaten by a dragon" and go on to find some way to test this hypothesis. Our presuppositions allow us only to consider other explanations: perhaps a satellite is passing between us and the moon.

As we begin to consider the claims of Christ in a world of religious pluralism, we first need to ask how such questions themselves are shaped by the presuppositions of our time and place. According to the presuppositions of large parts of our culture, some of these questions are not valid questions at all, any more than "What kind of dragon is swallowing the moon?" would be. In other parts of the world or at other times, people may have other unspoken assumptions, but for the moment our concern is the presuppositions of so-called "modern" culture.

The Trouble with Truth

The first thing we can see is that the term "truth" itself is not as popular as it once was. Consider the type of questions to which we might most readily respond, "That's true." Daily matters of observation or gossip surely qualify. Has a neighbor been writing bad checks? Unfortunately, it is true, for we received one ourselves. We still say quite confidently that two plus two equals four, and we accept the word of the quiz show host who tells us John Adams was the second president. Such things are true.

In other areas, however, the notion of truth is decidedly out of favor. The first is the area of personal relationships. It is not just that we rarely hear comments like, "He was untrue to her." People question whether love belongs in the realm of truth at all.

According to the presuppositions of our time, it is almost impossible to lie by saying "I love you," since love has to do with emotions and desires which are in themselves neither true or false, right or wrong. One person may not be feeling the same thing as another when he or she says it; this is obviously a very subjective decision. If we defined love as "willing the best for the one loved," it would seem that there would be a more objective basis for deciding whether love were "true" or not. Nevertheless, we shall see that this runs into difficulty because terms like "best" are also thought to be subjective.

A second area is that of morality. Our age is much less ready than previous ones to attribute truth to moral judgments. Past generations were rich in maxims which purported to express moral truths, such as "Honesty is the best policy." Today, however, we stress that in certain situations lying may be the best of the possible alternatives. The real truth or validity of a moral judgment cannot be decided by the content of the behavior itself (lying, stealing) but must be decided by the goals and results of the behavior. Lying to save a life may be a supremely moral act. Determination of the truth of a moral judgment must take into account the ultimate horizon against which it is made, the ultimate goal it serves.

Curiously, then, the third area—that of goals and ultimate beliefs—is precisely the one where truth has become most unfashionable. It is in the realm of ultimate commitment that modern thought has most vigorously disputed the category of "truth." One's ultimate may be the dialectic of history (Marxism), the glory of God, the service of others, the will to power, or escape from the illusion of a "self." These are guiding principles through which various people have found meaning in life. Something like these may even be necessary for a full and healthy human life. None, however, can be supposed to be *true* to the exclusion of the others, except in the purely personal sense that it is the one that works best for you at present.

Personal relationships and moral judgments were once thought to be areas where we could seek, if not certainly find, objective truth. Now, however, these areas are thought to be judged only by reference to ultimate goals and principles. Yet none of these goals is itself true or false. Thus each refers itself for verification to the next higher one, but in terms of truth the buck never stops anywhere. Sometimes love is proposed as the ultimate guiding principle by which the truth of all other choices or actions may be judged, but this only brings us full circle to the deep confusion over whether love has anything objective about it or is purely subjective.

These views are pervasive in our society, affecting the presuppositions of Christians and non-Christians alike. They are part of the intellectual air we breathe, even though we may feel they are fundamentally mistaken. They are crucial to our approach to the claims of Christ, because these claims fall into the three areas just discussed.

When we confess "Jesus is Lord," we are talking about: (1)

a personal relationship to Jesus Christ, (2) the affirmation of certain values, and (3) the truth of one among many competing descriptions of our human situation. No wonder, then, when Christians speak of Jesus Christ as the way, the truth, and the life, they find themselves increasingly at odds with persons around them.

Roots of the Question

How did we get to this point? The answer to such a question requires a history of the past few centuries. It is not difficult to note some of the primary forces which have altered our presuppositions regarding truth.

The first of these is the rise of science. Knowledge gained through science has affected our perception of truth. Geology and anthropology have extended our horizons far into the past. Astronomy and physics take us to the outer edges of a universe which expands for unimaginably vast distances and to the inner world at the subatomic level with its inconceivably minute particles. Our awareness of a very small portion of the vast whole tends to inhibit many of us from claiming truth for ideas or beliefs which, after all, come only from this small corner of the universe.

Probably more influential than supposed implications of simple scientific facts has been the impact of scientific method. No scientist is supposed to claim finality for the results of research. The scientist is expected to remain always open to revision or refutation. To be sure, there has been ample demonstration that scientists do not in fact always behave this way, but the image of the scientist who supposedly takes nothing on faith and withholds complete conviction has had a deep effect.

A second influence has been an awareness of history. Historical study has brought recognition that, just as the ancient Sumerians or Aztecs assumed without question certain beliefs which are strange to us, so we by virtue of being born into our own society wear a certain type of spectacles through which we see the world. We see everything through these spectacles, though we can within limits study their distortions and correct our vision. As we have realized this, it has seemed more and more dubious that any person, teaching, or event conditioned by one historical age could offer a final truth for all times and persons. Our growing knowledge of the historical setting of the Bible has been no exception.

A third important influence has been increased study of and acquaintance with the major faiths of the world. Until quite recently, direct contact with another faith in its own cultural setting was the experience of only a few. Such contact is more common now, however, and careful study of other faiths has become well established.

The result has been an increasing application of the category of "religion" to a wide variety of studies. This, of course, involves placing Christianity in a row alongside the other objects of study. For a substantial part of the modern period the Christian West had been able to dictate the terms under which other religions were compared with Christianity. This usually meant that the best of Christian ideals were contrasted with the worst practices of other faiths. Our new situation has made that comparison increasingly less plausible.

Such study has increased our appreciation of the strengths and virtues of other faiths and encouraged a proper humility among Christians. Nevertheless, we must also recognize that the effort to move beyond the study of other specific faiths, their beliefs and practices, to the study of "religion" itself remains very confused. Having put all these things in a row—Confucian moral order, animist ritual, Hindu mysticism, Christian historical proclamation, Muslim theocracy—we have difficulty explaining why they all belong in the same row.

Any thread which connects them all must, it seems, be extended to include many other philosophies, such as Marxism, humanism, or even nationalism. These things, too, provide a structure of meaning, an ultimate world view. Such is usually the kind of definition of religion given in textbooks of religion. Even to say that religion has to do with relations between humans and the divine or the sacred says a good deal too much, since the word "divine" means dramatically different things to a Buddhist and a Christian, for instance.

Despite these problems, it has become common to view religions as something of which there are various brands, one of them being Christianity. This approach has had its impact on the idea of religious truth. Before, different faiths had been seen as different things. They are now seen as different forms of the same thing. Once the new outlook becomes a presupposition, the question of truth undergoes a vast change, for we do not ordinarily apply the categories "true/false" to forms of the same thing. For example, we may distinguish between true ice cream and imitation or false ice cream, but we do not seriously debate whether chocolate or vanilla is the true ice cream.

Finally, and perhaps practically most important of all among the forces of change, there is what we might call the bad conscience of Western humanity.[1] We are painfully aware that the confident proclamation of final truths in the past has included the claim of racial superiority and the right of Western whites to rule others "for their own good." And among these conventional truths which seemed so obvious to earlier generations was also the conviction that Christianity was the one true faith.

Racism, economic exploitation, and sexual discrimination all flourished to some extent in the shadow of these convictions. The voices of those injured by these evils finally made clear to us how badly the "Christian West" had betrayed the principles of the gospel. Hoping to learn at least one lesson, our culture now shies away from anything that might fuel renewed charges of Western arrogance. Others are ready to remind us, even when we are not, that there is plenty of good reason to have a bad conscience.

The West remains the richest and most developed part of the world. The rest of the world continues to seek what the West has, in technology, education, freedom, skills, culture. In such a situation it is doubly difficult to avoid charges of arrogance, especially as those who seek what the West has are often resentful of the necessity to do so. They feel that the riches, literal and figurative, which they want must somehow have been stolen from them, since the West does not have them by any special virtue or superiority.

It is not my purpose to argue the validity of these views, but only to point out their impact. It seems very oppressive to say that the West has the truth in science and technology and medicine and *also* to suggest that it has the supreme religious truth as well. If the West is at the moment leading in the first areas, should it perhaps be assumed that the East is superior in the second? The East certainly has the more ancient religious traditions. So the stereotypes of the "spiritual East" and the "materialistic West" have become prominent—despite strong spiritual traditions in the West and many material achievements of the East.

There is, of course, no logical reason why we in the West might not have repented more of our science and philosophy (both deeply implicated in the racism and colonialism of the past) than of our Christian faith. Computers do not solve all problems. The best water treatment plant may in some cases be one that uses natural or traditional technology rather than high-tech equipment. Less-developed lands may have much in the realm of practical wisdom to contribute as well as to receive.

A cynic might note that the export of technology is financially profitable, but the export of faith is not. Less cynically, we may say that some Western achievements, at least, in health care or agriculture, are true goods which ought to be shared with others. At any rate, it is worth a moment's reflection to consider whether it is not a grave mistake for both sides to suppose so readily that the West has the answers to all really practical questions and to none that are religious.

In this atmosphere Western thought (and especially Christianity—the "Western religion") must bear the burden. In intellectual circles it has become rather conventional to compensate for the practical dominance of the West by relativizing any of its religious claims to truth. At times it seems that people wish to attribute as many as possible of the West's past sins to a "dogmatic" Christianity—so that, in disavowing that faith, they can believe themselves rid of the sins. With this scapegoat they can avoid addressing the true sources of those sins and the material sacrifice which might go with giving them up, whether the sins are racism, greed, or cultural imperialism.

For Christians who want the gospel to be heard, one way out of this situation is clear. We need to work toward ending the overwhelming dominance of the West in the material and economic realm. We know it is not God's will that the majority of the world's people should be hungry and destitute. If we could improve the material well-being of the rest of the world, we would overcome one of the major obstacles to evangelism *here* in our Western culture. There would no longer be this implicit need to downplay or denigrate Christian belief. This is only one of the many ways in which our mandates to both personal and social witness for Christ support each other.

Christians surely must share in repentance for the sins of Western nations acting as "Christian countries." Indeed, the bad conscience of the Christian West may be viewed in some measure as a Christian phenomenon. Some world faiths seem less guilt-stricken by their failings than others. Islam, for instance, was at least as deeply implicated in the African slave trade as Christianity, but has never experienced the same level of shame over this fact. Depending on one's place inside or outside these faiths, this difference may be seen either as a moral failing or a healthier acceptance of life's realities.

As Christians we do not believe that the past sins of the West followed necessarily from the presence of Christianity. Certainly, however, recognition of and repentance for them *should* follow in cultures influenced at all by Christianity. If this humility shapes our encounter with other religions, this is a good thing. A certain inhibition in testifying to the truth of Christian faith may in fact stem from an acute sense of our failure to live up to our Lord's calling. This, too, is healthy. But none of these factors or the cultural presuppositions we have mentioned ought to keep us from presenting Christ's claims.

Some Examples of Cultural Presuppositions

It may be useful at this point to provide some concrete examples of the attitudes I have mentioned. One of the most familiar is the assertion that an individual's Christian belief is not based on the truth or validity of the Christian gospel, but upon whether or not one's parents are Christians. If they are not, and one is a believer, faith is said to stem from rebellion against them, or from living in a (supposedly) Christian culture, or perhaps from some psychological need.

Most often in our culture, comments like these are connected with the presupposition that there is no religious truth. They offer explanations of how and why we could come to believe what is not so. They assume that Christ is not the only savior and explain why someone would believe that he is. The problem with this approach is that before you can explain *why* someone is wrong, you first have to show that she or he *is* wrong.

The error of a position is most often simply presumed. This is a very popular modern game.[2] We are accustomed to explaining other people's beliefs by reference to their economic class, their race, their sex, their nationality. We do not argue that their statements are false; we simply point out some reason why they might want to believe what they are saying, and so dismiss their belief.

The game is often played in the names of certain intellectual giants like Freud and Marx, who offered profound analyses of our psychological and social motivations. But these thinkers are open to the same fundamental objection. They explained functions that faith could perform even if it were, in Freud's word, an "illusion," but they never demonstrated that faith *was* an illusion. Some people have played the same game with Freud and Marx, explaining why they *had* to regard religion as an illusion. This whole mode of argument, which either discredits all beliefs or none at all, indicates how much questions of truth are avoided.

A different type of example is provided by a radio program I heard not too long ago. It was a documentary in which several young evangelical women were interviewed. One in particular was quite striking in the sincerity and humility of her testimony as to what her faith in Christ had meant to her: greater self-esteem, new hope, and fulfillment.

The two women interviewing her were troubled, however. They pressed her in regard to this faith in Christ. They agreed that it seemed good to her. But, they asked, she did not think, did she, that it was objectively true, true for everyone? Yes, she replied, in fact, she did. One of the interviewers, a religion professor, seized upon this. As though explaining something to a child, she told the young woman that such an idea was inherently imperialistic and led to the persecution of others. It was a dangerous thing. Such ideas of truth have to be outgrown (not disproved, significantly), the professor said, if we are to live safely together.

The young woman did not say, though she well might have, "It must not be so terrible a thing to maintain that something is true, since you, after all, are doing it right now." This was precisely so. The professor believed there was no universal truth in the realm of faith. She believed that this belief itself was universally true. She was out to convince and convert others to this view. The interviewer was as imperialistic and dogmatic as any missionary that could be imagined. *The only difference was that her truth was that there must be no truth.*

The general level of evangelism in our society has not diminished. People are as ready as ever to adopt beliefs and defend them. But the way to "sell" your position is not to argue its truth. Instead, you deny any dogmatic interest in objective truth and commend your point of view as functionally practical in some way, the more general the way the better. Perhaps the prime example of this is the evangelism for certain types of oriental meditation on the grounds that it helps you do *whatever* you want to do, only better.

In other words, all truths which we wish to get others to accept are commended as "neutral," effective *means*, rather than as debatable, objective *ends*. Even in our political debates, there is an attempt to avoid moral or objective categories and to press one's preferred truth in purely functional terms. Our best-selling books tell us how to get flat stomachs, long lives, and freedom from the constraints of money or of other people. They do not argue what healthy, long-lived, capable humans themselves are for. That would be dogmatic.

Finally we may take an example which brings us directly to the topic we are most concerned with. One prominent theologian was heard to say to another, in reference to Christian claims for Christ, "You can't say those things any more. Other religions are all around us, in our midst." This statement is rather typical in many quarters, but it is a strange statement. Most major faiths have been around longer than Christianity. It would be more appropriate to say that Christianity has been in *their* midst. In any case, if the statement is really referring to geography, it means that you ought not to say in people's hearing what you say in private. Simple hypocrisy!

On the other hand it might be a way of saying that we now recognize it was *never* right to say such things. This is a rather strong statement. It says the first Christians and the New Testament writers were mistaken. Even more, it is saying that *we* ought not to be Christians, since we are the product of missionary movements based on those things that can't be said. The conclusion of this line of reasoning is that no one should be a Christian.

Most commonly this statement is taken to mean that while it might have been all right to say and believe these things in the past, it is no longer right. This does not suggest that those who are Christians should abandon their faith, but does it mean that certain things were once true but are not so any longer? Or that they remain true but ought not to be mentioned? Or that they were never true, but were once necessary to believe?

The most sense that can be made of this claim is to suppose that these statements about the unique saving significance of Christ were a *form* in which Christians once expressed their faith, and now must give way to different forms. Of course this presumes that the real content of Christian faith does not have to do with the decisive significance of Christ. Furthermore, it presumes to know what this true content is, behind the forms in which it is expressed. But such presumptions must be defended and argued, not just assumed.

Is Christian Faith an Accident?

In other words, some people suggest that Christians are mistaken about the true content of their own faith. What they think to be the heart of the matter is in fact only a historically conditioned form, really an accident. The New Testament speaks of Jesus as a savior who died for our sins. What if "savior" and "sin" are only culturally conditioned ways of talking and do not truly describe what Jesus was and did at all?

People in that earlier culture had such ideas, according to this view. Being very attached to Jesus and quite excited about some experiences they had with him, they used this language to talk about him and what he meant to them. If they had been Africans, or Chinese, or twentieth-century Americans, however, they would have used quite different language and ideas to refer to the same objective events. If Christianity had moved eastward instead of westward, for instance, it is claimed that Jesus would have become an *avatar* or *bodhisattva* figure, and we would not have these "exclusivistic" ideas in Christian theology.

It is not just that the biblical witnesses used conditioned ideas, according to the philosophy we are discussing. Conditioned ideas can still express truth. This argument goes further and suggests that the language and images used to describe Christ and the events surrounding him were fundamentally "out of sync" with what they described.

There is a certain plausibility to this view. It is true that an isolated people who had never seen a camera, and who saw a Polaroid snapshot of one of their number, might describe the taking of the picture as the "capture of someone's soul." We may say this is a mistake. The event is of a different order than the description, however. It is more complex but less mysterious than the description implies. The description explains the event in language we do not view as appropriate to it: supernatural or spiritual language for a physical, technical event. The people describe the picture-taking in these terms because these are the only terms they have.

So, some English theologians have argued in a recent controversial book, the early Christians thought of God as incarnate in Christ because that was the only "tool," the only category they had at hand to deal with this extraordinary person.[3] This category, which was an arbitrary accident of their time and situation, was hardened by the church into a dogmatic description of what actually happened. This, they say, was all a terrible mistake.

Now, in the first place, there appears to be no reason to believe that if Christianity had developed in another culture Christ would have been a less exclusive figure. In fact Christianity *did* move eastward at a very early date. Not only did it reach India, but it was isolated there, having very little interchange with Christians in the West. The result was not an *avatar* Jesus, one more face among the many of divinity, but a Christ who retained a unique status.[4]

The early Christians had a rich pluralism of religious language and options open to them. If they had wished to make Jesus an *avatar*, they had an example close at hand in the cults of the mother goddess who went by different names in different locations.[5] There would have been real political advantage in adopting such an approach as well, for it would have made Christians much more compatible with the world around them, and thus they would have avoided persecution.

In the second place, both Jews and Gentiles did not just apply ready-made ideas to Jesus. Instead they pressed to a quite uncommon extreme the ideas which were available to them. The idea that Yahweh, the jealous God of the Jews, of whom no image could be made and whose name was not to be spoken, should become incarnate in a human being, was not an idea that was simply "lying around."

These early Christians give every indication of knowing that their concepts were inadequate to what they were describing. They seem to have sensed problems with the literalness of their language, but the problems they sensed were that this language said too little, not too much.

Suppose what can in no way be ruled out—that the reality was, as nearly as can be described, what the New Testament describes. How else would these people, in that time and place, describe an actual resurrection from the dead, for example? Unless we are to assume from the beginning that such a thing cannot happen (in which case, why bother with the evidence and descriptions at all?), we have to say that this is the way it would be described.

On the basis of the description *alone* it is impossible to know which is the case: an appropriate description of an extraordinary reality, or a culturally distorted description of an ordinary reality. The fact that they had some material with which they could construct an account of God becoming human does not mean it did not happen—any more than our imagination and technical ability to describe a space flight to the moon means that the Apollo missions are mythical.

A Place to Stand

We have taken this time to speak of the general intellectual atmosphere of our culture, because the presuppositions of this atmosphere determine how the question of Christ and pluralism is generally understood. Plainly the context in which the question is treated is very important. What standpoint should we take?

On the one hand, we could stand outside of faith altogether. We could assess Christ from a perspective which sees religion purely in terms of some other human endeavor. We might see religion as a primitive form of science and evaluate Christ as a step forward, but one long since surpassed. We might say religion has to do with emotions and argue over whether Jesus represents the purest appeal to our highest feelings, producing most perfectly the sensibilities of worship. Then again, we might regard religion as a support for moral and social values and consider whether Jesus gives us the highest and most absolute values, whether his example and teachings are the standard for the fullest human life. In all these cases, we would begin with some idea of what religion is in general—apart from what it *claims* to be—and we would use this ruler to measure Jesus.

Another approach would be to try to study the question in a neutral way, without assuming *any* standard of what is better or worse. Here we would explore the affirmations of the various faiths in the spirit of the parable of a king who put an elephant in the midst of a group of blind people. Each thought the elephant something different, according to which part the individual touched. We could investigate the reality of the whole, which all faiths perceive in part, and see how Jesus' part relates to the others. This approach, however, has a serious flaw, which is reflected in the parable. It assumes that we are in the position of the king, the sighted person among the blind. It presumes that we know the one reality which the blind people touch only in different parts.

But *how* do we know this? If there is some direct path to knowledge other than that taken by various faiths, it ought to be shared and tested. In fact, however, the person who takes this "neutral" standpoint has no special path to knowledge, no sighted eyes as opposed to the blindness of others. The stance of neutrality is often just such a disguised presupposition.

Someone might say that we could build up an idea of religious reality by putting together what we find in common among all religions. This approach runs into severe difficulties, however. What is the common ground? Even if it could be found, what is abstracted from all religions belongs to none; it is not a living faith but an artificial creation. It has no stronger claim than any of the others.

On the other hand, perhaps we could at least rule *out* some religious beliefs or practices (like human sacrifice) on the basis of the consensus of *most* religious belief. But what sample will we poll for the consensus? Religious beliefs in our time? Over all time? If the consensus changes with the passage of time, will our standards change too? Are we committed to the notion that truth in matters of faith is the same as the majority opinion?

It is certainly possible to study different faiths without being a believer. One can describe points of conflict or similarity between faiths, and evaluate them. But it is not possible to do this from a standpoint which is totally uncommitted.

We are often deceived by the fact that we can perceive blatant prejudice and bias in personal preferences. Because we can see this prejudice so clearly, we assume we can reach a point of "no prejudice" by progressively eliminating personal preferences, cultural influences, and so on. But this is an arithmetical delusion. It is like supposing that, if cutting our hair shorter improves our appearance, we will be most attractive if we cut if all off.

We cannot reach the point of truly neutral objectivity. Beliefs and convictions are not just objects to be eliminated; they are instruments with which we work and live. The "impartial" jury is not *totally* impartial. Its members are in fact partial to truth and justice. They just do not happen to be partial to either of the parties before them. When we hope to find a disinterested judge to deal with our case, we are not looking for one who could not care less about the issues. We want intense interest, but of the right sort. Unfortunately, however, we have no perfect thermometer for measuring the right kind of interest where truth in matters of faith or morals or politics is concerned.

We tend to say automatically that those whose interest is based on a personal need are prejudiced and nonobjective. At the same time, however, we recognize that those with particular needs—the poor, the oppressed, the hungry, the orphaned—may be privileged to see certain truths about our system and our world that others cannot. Perhaps their testimony is not discredited by this need, but enhanced by it. In a similar way we may question the popular readiness to disparage religious faith because some people with personal problems or needs often turn to it. We would not doubt that there was water in a particular place because we had heard of it only from people who get thirsty!

Whatever standpoint we choose for judging the claims of different faiths, we must acknowledge that this position itself involves commitments and can be subjected to criticism. This does not mean that judgment is impossible or truth irrelevant in the realm of faith. We can judge different faiths on the basis of their consistency with their *own* stated authorities (Scripture or tradition, for instance). We can judge them according to standards of reason and morality, which will primarily have to do with whether or not the faith in question truly pictures and actually meets the human situation in its personal, social, and metaphysical dimensions. Indeed, one of the standards by which we may judge faiths is the extent to which they themselves support and are consistent with universal standards of judgment. Personal need may not discredit our choice of a particular faith, but its claims to truth are advanced insofar as we can argue and defend it as more than *only* a purely individual preference.

It is a curious prejudice to suppose that religious questions can be decided correctly only by those with no religious beliefs or commitments. Of course, Christians have certain motives for wanting to arrive at certain answers, just as those of other faiths or of no faith have motives for wanting to arrive at different answers. No one is pure in that sense. Yet, all things considered, religious commitment seems rather an advantage than a disqualification.

To have some personal experience of or felt need for salvation may make you prejudiced. Without such experience or need, however, how can one even intelligently study or understand any of the major faiths? Perhaps, as the saying goes, "the person who knows only one religion knows none." But to know *none* in any but the totally abstract sense is even worse.

It would seem, then, that the best standpoint for addressing the question of Christ and pluralism, or any faith claim, is one that stands within a *particular* faith commitment but is willing to evaluate and explore that commitment in universal terms. This means discussing and evaluating the faith commitment in terms which are open to participation of those from other perspectives and commitments.

For our purposes this means that we address the claims of Christ as Christians, but that we do not appeal exclusively to warrants that only Christians will accept. We look to consistency with our own authority—Scripture—but also to consistency with reason and human experience.

True Pluralism

Talk of pluralism can easily become very sloppy. To some people it means the acceptance of *one* of the competing versions of the truth: the one which says all faiths are forms of the same thing. There is one essence, but it has different outward appearances. To say the United States is a "pluralistic" nation in this interpretation would mean that although some of us are black, some of us speak Spanish at home, some of us come from Native American tribes; underneath all these superficial differences we are or will become of one character: Americans. We accept others of different appearances because we see that underneath they are just like us.

But pluralism in a true sense means that we live with each other and accept each other though we see clearly that we are *not* the same. America is a pluralistic nation, not because underneath cosmetic appearances we all think and feel and act the same, but because we do not. There are real differences in our families, our histories, and our convictions about ultimate matters.

True pluralism does not mean coming to terms with my Buddhist neighbor by affirming that underneath it all we believe exactly the same thing. If that is so, we are not really distinct and plural. Pluralism means living with real distinctions, conflicting answers about what is most determinative for our lives.

Very often today it is toleration and not true pluralism which seems most influential. Such an approach has become very popular in the West because of its apparent tolerance for other views. All religions are said to be seeking the same thing; any number of different beliefs may serve to lead to the essence of religion.

The goodwill of this sentiment does not stand up to close examination. Its outward respect for all faiths is in fact a patronizing arrogance toward them. To tell the Muslim that she or he is seeking the same thing as the Hindu is not likely to be regarded as a compliment. The presumption that we know what a religion and its believers are *really* about better than they do themselves, is one we are free to make and to defend as best we can. Nevertheless, it does not indicate either a high regard for the other faith or a commitment to true pluralism.

The idea that all existing religious beliefs and symbols are expressions of some reality, which is filtered through all these contradictory masks, makes of that reality itself a cosmic zero. It is the great everything—or nothing, the night in which all cats are gray. Since this undefined reality can be encountered through the use of any and all practices and symbols, we cannot know or speak of its character or its relation to human values and behavior.

The first and one of the most important steps in discussing "Christ and pluralism," then, will be to be sure we agree on what is meant by pluralism. If it is the "ice cream" pluralism we have just outlined, where differences of faith are like different flavors of ice cream, then the question of Christ and pluralism is not a question at all. Any exclusive claim for Christ is ruled out to begin with.

True pluralism on the other hand does not assume that all can be melted into the same basic substance. It leaves open the possibility that some faiths, at least, might be forms of the same thing. It does not rule this out, but it does not assume it either. Rather than supposing that real differences are dangerous, and ought to be defused from the very beginning, true pluralism will allow that we may differ even over issues of the greatest importance.

I accept the affirmations of the major faiths about their distinctives as trustworthy; they point to real differences. I presume that there is a way to live in love with these differences, without distorting anyone's faith or falling into violence or coercion.

Perhaps all religions are, in some as yet unproven way, the same. Or, even though they are not the same, perhaps we must *pretend* they are to keep from each other's throats. That is possible, but, on the basis of the evidence, I do not think it is true. There is no reason to presuppose that Christianity is just another religion alongside others, as there is no reason to suppose that Hinduism is just another religion alongside others.

A philosophy student was once told by his teacher: "I'll say this for you; you can see the obvious." This is an important and underrated skill. One thing that is obvious is that, however readily we may list what we call "religions," they appear to be (and tenaciously struggle to be) different. They have their own identities. Were they individually to accept the idea that they are not essentially different, they would cease to exist. That some people look forward to just this event marks them as devotees of yet an additional faith, which might as well itself be added to the list.

However long we may want to put the question of truth on the back burner, while studying each faith, understanding it, comparing and contrasting it, the question still remains to be dealt with. Certain presuppositions prevalent in our particular culture and time may discourage us from dealing with it, but that is a result of historical circumstance—and circumstance is not sufficient to decide whether Jesus Christ is the way, the truth, and the life.

Red Herrings

We have looked briefly at presuppositions that often stand in the way of any consideration of Jesus Christ as universal Savior. Just beyond these presuppositions we are likely to encounter a set of arguments that attempt to close the case as soon as it can be pried open. But at least they are arguments, and the conversation has begun. In this chapter I want to survey what I will call, to borrow from the detective story, red herrings.

These are arguments which try to divert the focus from the truth or falsehood of Christian claims about Christ to some other topic. I do not mean to suggest that the questions raised in this way are not worthy of discussion in their own place. My concern is the role they often play as screens to ward off Christian claims. I simply want to say enough here to indicate that, however interesting they may be, their substance is not sufficient to rule out Christian affirmations.

A New Problem or an Old One?

One of the first things we are likely to hear about the problem of Christ and pluralism today is that it is new and unprecedented. We are told that Christians must give up the claim of exclusiveness in their ideas of Jesus, for the sudden lightning of modernity has cast everything into a new and vivid perspective. We are in a new day and must think in a new way. We know about other religions. We understand how faith can function at times as a front for selfish personal and social ends.

Our age is indeed unlike any other before it. So too, we tend to forget, was the age before ours unlike any before it. But the set of questions which have to do with Christ as only one among many options is not so totally new as is sometimes loosely implied. Pluralism is not an entirely new experience for Christianity; it originated in a Graeco-Roman world which had a rich variety of religions and quasi-religious philosophies.

The first centuries of the church were marked by familiarity with other faiths. The converts who made up the church brought with them backgrounds in Manicheanism, Mithraism, Stoicism, Neoplatonism, Zoroastrianism, the cults of Isis and Cybele, German tribal religions, or Celtic mysteries. The early Christians had worshiped at many different altars.

As a group they probably had much more firsthand experience with other faiths than most Christians today, certainly most western Christians. The fact that the earliest Christians were all Jews ought not to blind us to the fact that very soon the church was drawn mostly from Gentiles. In terms of religious background, these new converts were a very mixed bag.

Nor are present solutions to the problem of pluralism entirely new. The classical age also felt the appeal of the notion that in religion as in politics, "all roads lead to Rome." As behind all governors and client kings, however different, stood Roman power and the Roman emperor, so it might be speculated that the gods themselves wore different local faces.

Certainly a good many of the ancients were ready to consider the idea that others worshiped the same gods as they under different names, that Isis in Egypt was Ishtar in Babylon. People who traveled about the ancient world were likely in religion to follow the motto "When in Rome, do as the Romans do." A certain respect paid to the local gods was both polite and prudent. At Rome itself there was a temple called the

Pantheon, where images of the various gods and goddesses were lodged. Christ, too, would have been more than welcome there.

Christians first made themselves obnoxious, we might say, by refusing this kind of solution. They insisted that to place Christ in that honorable assembly was to misunderstand totally the choice that Christ presented. In this refusal they followed in the footsteps of their mother faith. The Jews had no image that could be put in the Pantheon, and they steadfastly resisted the enlightened suggestion that the one they worshiped was only another face of Olympian Zeus.

The prickliness of the religion question was in a sense invented by Israel and carried on by Christians. Of course religious groups had clashed and fought before, violently and regularly. A strange religion was as good an excuse to hate one's neighbor as a strange race. The two, in fact, were often inseparable. Devotion to one's own mystery or cult might be demonstrated quite directly by vandalizing someone else's. This ugly psychology is, unhappily, not extinct today.

A student of early religions may suspect that this animosity was not rooted in notions of truth and falsehood so much as in ties of blood, city, or race: "I reject your god not because it is not real [often other peoples' gods were seen as dangerously real] but because it is yours." One of the charges brought against the Greek philosopher Socrates when he was tried by the city of Athens was that he did not believe in the gods of his own city. This was a religious offense, but perhaps much more a political one: treason.

What was puzzling about Jews and Christians to their contemporaries was precisely this point. They were not surprised that Jews and Christians rejected gods and cults other than their own, but that they rejected them as *false*. Worship of the Roman emperor as a god was not a very deep-rooted faith even among Romans, much less their subjects. Although most people had little use for this interloper in the more intense circle of their local religion, they usually were quite willing to offer the minimal sacrifice. Done and forgotten! Except for the Jews and the Christians.

People could understand refusal to recognize gods on the ground that they belonged to other cities or tribes or professions, but they were surprised at rejection on general principle. It is extremely hard to know just what sort of existence the ancients attributed to their gods, but it seems clear that Jews and Christians attributed a new kind of nonexistence to gods they did not worship. When the Jews took this attitude, its effect was limited by the fact that it was the view of one race or nation. With Christianity, however, the idea spread like windblown seed in the rest of the empire. For such "atheism" both Jews and Christians paid dearly.

Christians practiced a more vigorous pluralism. They took other gods seriously enough not to patronize them but to deny them. We conventionally say that Christian martyrs died to witness to Christ—and so they did. One could also say, however, that they died of taking other faiths more seriously than was common, seriously enough to refuse even a superficial assent to them. We must also be honest enough to say that, when eventually Christians came uppermost in the state, they would on occasion take matters of faith seriously enough not only to die but to kill.

As Christianity triumphed in the West, carrying with it the legacy of Greek philosophy, this claim to truth in matters of faith became part of Western culture. This is why it was within the sphere of Christianity, and there alone, that many persons turned to the radical negation of religion and of Christianity itself.

In secularism the kind of denial that Christianity had pioneered against others was turned against Christianity and, as was naively supposed, against all forms of faith. This, too, was a new thing under the sun. The unique approach to human faith known as the philosophy of religion—the reasoned evaluation of the truth in religious beliefs—arose only in the West.

Outside the monotheistic faiths of the near East (Judaism, Christianity, Islam), this idea of exclusive truth was never accepted in the same way. The Buddhist and the Hindu believe in the *validity* of their paths, but not to the exclusion of others. They see true and false, right and wrong, as categories to be transcended—polarities, like the negative and positive poles of a battery which generate energy to make the world go 'round. Thus the evil experienced by those on the lowest rungs of the caste system, for instance, is regarded as "bad" only in a certain perspective. From another, it is a necessary part of the path of purgation that leads to a higher status in the next reincarnation and eventually to a hoped-for release.

"Right belief" and conversion do not play the same roles in these faiths as in monotheistic religions. It is not so much that there is a wrong way and a right way. There is only one way. "False" beliefs or "bad" acts will have automatic consequences in the cycles of rebirth, but they do not definitively change anything.

Today we hear many voices commending the Eastern approach to truth and attacking the rigid, dogmatic cast of the Western idea of truth, which is influenced by Christianity. Such rigidity is a kind of mental sickness, we are told, like compulsively arranging things in rows. By the same reasoning, it was a very bad mistake when Jews insisted on being so rigid about who God was and was not, and when Christians followed suit. This, say the critics, has been the root of numberless evils, since assumed possession of *the* truth leads to intolerance and aggression.

On the face of it, this is a strange argument, since there is plenty of empirical evidence available about the exclusivist behavior of cultures shaped by what are said to be nonexclusive faiths. The more relaxed view of truth supposedly found in the East has been quite at home there with the most rigid and authoritarian of social structures. Buddhist countries have not lacked for their crusades, some pitting monks against each other. Vietnam and Cambodia offer long histories of oppression and intolerance. The bloodshed between Hindus and Buddhists in places like Sri Lanka is well known.

None of this proves Christianity is the true faith, as Christianity has its own sins. But, since much of the world has been able to wreak at least equal havoc without benefit of an exclusive faith, it would seem that there ought to be some hesitation about the commonplace assertion that commitment to exclusive religious truth is the root of such social evils.

We must also recognize that the rigidity of this approach to truth undergirds our understandings of the moral imperative for human rights and justice. Apart from an exclusive center of value and worship, a jealous God, there could be no rejection of idols, no unconditional rejection of certain evils. Many of the attitudes of social concern we take for granted in the West grow out of this soil.

In short, the present discussion of pluralism is not totally new. We are hardly the first to know that pluralism exists. Insofar as the problem of pluralism means a conflict among various truth claims, it has arisen partly as a *result* of Christianity, as I have pointed out.

Certainly our world is different from that of the early church. We cannot think as though we lived before certain determinative events of our age like the Holocaust or Hiroshima. Though the question of pluralism was not invented yesterday, it has a special shape and urgency in our day.

The question is not whether an unprecedented new dilemma requires us to throw off an old, outmoded view of truth in faith. Rather, it is whether we ought to abandon the singular approach to truth which has arisen in the sphere of Judaism and Christianity. Should we abandon it in favor of a revised form of the oldest approach to such differences? Do we need a sort of *realpolitik* of religion, in which other people's gods are accepted or rejected not because they are true or false, right or wrong, but because they are *theirs*? And if the numbers of the followers be sufficient, do we admit any faith to the club wherein all are equals?

Missionaries: Bane or Blessing?

We may turn now to perhaps the most common issue raised to dismiss the claims of Christ: the sins of the missionaries. The line of thought can be quickly summarized. If the missionary movement was a great evil, and if it was produced by belief in Christ's unique lordship, then this belief ought to be avoided.

Such a view depends on two questionable assumptions. The first is that, if some missionaries were blameworthy, all must be. The second is that the missionary movement was basically evil. In many circles the latter will be assumed without comment, usually in vast ignorance of the history of that movement. We need not romanticize missionaries in order to reject this conventional cartoon.

The popular view of the missionary, even among many Christians, is of a dour, pinched person who imposed a grim theology on innocent people while supporting colonial exploitation of their land as "God's will." This person was supposedly concerned mainly to stifle the healthy sexuality of native peoples and to increase corporate profits.

This simplistic picture is so well ingrained that we must take a moment to consider it. The first thing to note is that, curiously, it seems to be most deeply ingrained in the West. In countries which received the missionaries, one usually encounters a much more complex and favorable view of their influence. This is not to say that people in these countries, including the Christians, do not see sins in the mission history and resent them. They are also aware of the positive effects, however.

Each country is likely to have its own particular estimate of the strengths and failings of the mission movement there. Missionaries were not produced with a cookie cutter, nor were the cultures they entered. There is no simple way to tell a story so full of color, drama, and variety.

It is well to remember that the missionary, as this discussion pictures her or him, is a relatively new development. The church was a missionary church from the beginning, but after the prodigious growth and expansion of the first five centuries, the situation changed. From A.D. 500 to A.D. 1500 Christianity, in terms of the number of its adherents and its geographical extent, was relatively static. It is true that during this time Russia and northern Germany were converted, and missions may have reached even to China, but these gains were offset by the threat of extinction as the onrush of Islam swept it from the near East, North Africa, Asia Minor, Spain, and southern Italy. Three hundred years after the death of Mohammed, Muslim armies were at the gates of Rome. By then the Mediterranean, which had been the highway for the Christian gospel in the first five centuries, was controlled and almost ringed by Islam. In 1453 Constantinople fell to the Turks, admitting them to southeastern Europe, and only two centuries later would Moslem armies be turned back from Vienna. The missionary impulse remained strong over these centuries, but Christianity was also struggling for survival.

Only after the expansion of the European Christian nations into North and South America did Christianity and the "Christian West" assume the proportions we now know. When most people think of missionaries, they think of those who went out from this dominant culture in the eighteenth and nineteenth centuries. As products of a unified culture, many of these missionaries identified much, too much, of that culture with the faith they professed. This is not surprising. What is surprising is the extent to which so many of them rose above this limitation.

The missionary impulse has always been a part of Christianity. It was present long before colonialism arose, and it has continued long after colonialism has withered. For instance, Africa, the continent which most readily comes to mind as part of colonial empires, has almost totally thrown off the political if not all the economic ties of colonialism, but Christianity was not rejected along with the colonial rule. Instead it goes on, growing at a speedy pace. If the mission movement was considered simply a mask for colonialism, it appears to have a strangely independent life.

Missionaries are seen by some as front persons for imperialism, administering Christianity as spiritual anesthesia while Western powers operated to remove the wealth. There is a degree of truth to the charge. We know, for instance, that some missionaries in China served as translators and negotiators for Western business interests. Yet missionaries—sometimes the same ones—went to isolated and outcast groups whom no colonial power cared for because they offered neither wealth nor profit.

Mission history is also full of conflict between economic interests and the church. For some 250 years, until the British government took over full rule of India in 1858, the East India Company held sway there. Throughout that time the company was actively hostile to missionaries.[1] For long periods it forbade their presence at all, because it feared evangelism would stir up hostility to the West or that missionaries would object to certain practices of the company. In either case missionaries would be bad for business. So it was that William Carey, father of the modern missionary movement, began his career hiding as a fugitive to avoid deportation by the East India Company.

Often the missionaries came in the wake of other Westerners whose interests had been selfishly simple and direct. Such was the case in most of the Pacific islands, where whalers and traders had stopped for profit or pleasure. Here the missionaries were sometimes less popular with other Westerners than with the indigenous people, who welcomed their reforms. The example of the Pacific islands is a good one, since the picture traditionally popular in many minds is one of liberated Polynesian women and lusty Yankee seamen persecuted in their idyllic Eden by joyless missionaries. More recently, however, as women anthropologists have taken the time to speak to Polynesian *women* about this history, the picture which has emerged is rather different.[2]

The "Mother Hubbard" dresses have long been used as a stock example for those who mock the missionaries. They say that only a crabbed mind would introduce such a form of dress, prudish and ludicrous in the heat of the tropics. But the testimony of the women in that culture is that this form of dress was welcomed as a form of liberation, an affirmation of a woman's right to control her own body instead of being regarded as available to all comers. It was an instrument and a symbol of personhood and independence.

These are only brief glimpses into the missionary movement, intended to show that it cannot be evaluated in a simplistic way. Another brief glimpse was provided in a speech to the Sixth Assembly of the World Council of Churches. Speaking to the assembly of church delegates from around the world, Dr. Gopal Singh represented the observers from other world faiths.[3] As an Indian and as a Sikh, he spoke more emphatically than most Christians in the room would have dared to do, thanking Christians for what they had given to India: schools, medical knowledge, political institutions. He thanked Christians for awakening his people to the horror of certain of their customs, such as the immolation of widows. He also thanked them for giving many Indian peoples the gift of their own languages, by providing the first scripts, grammars, and codifications of them. He even expressed gratitude for the pioneering work of Christian scholars in recovering the history and traditions of Indian religions. He did not spare criticism of the missionaries' complicity in what was worst in colonialism. But he made one thing clear: Subtract the mission movement from the history of the last three hundred years and the world would be much worse, not much better. Colonialism would have been more horrible, not less. The peoples of the two-thirds of the world beyond the West would be less empowered, not more.

The balance sheet on the modern missionary movement will be totaled differently by different people. It will certainly vary according to their evaluation of its central aim: the conversion of people to faith in Jesus Christ. But even many of those whose distaste for this heart of the movement is extreme have acknowledged its many benefits. None have denied its sacrifices.

It would not be farfetched to say that in another half century the liberation movements and revolutions of our age, from the Russian revolution to others still to come, will have left a legacy with some of the same complexities as that of the missions movement. Their legacy will be as problematic, perhaps much more so, in regard to coercive conversions, violations of human rights, imperialism, and cultural arrogance. On the other hand, there will be many substantial benefits to show as well.

No more massive assault on a traditional culture could be made than that of Mao on the culture of China, or of Pol Pot on that of Cambodia. No one proposes the abolition of the universal goals of equality and justice because of the horrible acts committed by such movements in the name of lofty goals. No more can the history of the missionary movement, a history much richer than the parodies of it, be made grounds for the dismissal of the One it served.

Christ and Cultures

Very closely connected to the negative image of missionaries is the charge of cultural imperialism. Christ cannot be for all people, it is said, because Christianity itself is a Western faith and therefore to make people Christians is the same as trying to make them Western and white. Continuing, such critics reason that Christianity is incompatible with the true reality of other cultures, which have their own religions, appropriate to them.

Unfortunately, Christian missions have at times literally and figuratively gathered a black congregation around the picture of a white, blue-eyed Christ. The church has reproduced more of Western culture in other lands than is good for the health of either. Yet here, too, the missionary movement has dramatic examples on the other side. The very success of the Christian mission has produced a natural concern that the church in other cultures put down real roots in those cultures. The size and independence of churches in the Third World have reached such proportions that Christianity is now in fact numerically a non-Western religion. Africa and South America are the most Christian continents. The majority of the world's Christians are nonwhite.

This development recalls another obvious fact. Christianity is not a Western religion. It comes from the Middle East. Its first believers were Semites. One of its early strongholds was North Africa, and another was Asia Minor. It grew and flourished in the West, but it also grew and mingled with other cultural streams in Russia, Byzantium, Lebanon, Ethiopia, Egypt, and India.

It is not only Westerners who were or who are missionaries. Like the earliest evangelists who came from the Middle East and Africa, non-European missionaries have won many to Christ, usually persons of their own race. In the Pacific islands for instance, the work was largely carried on by the people themselves. Today the so-called "daughter" churches of Western missions are not only largely independent, but are themselves sending missionaries to other lands, including the Western nations. The Christian missionary corps is increasingly multicultural. Third World mission agencies have more than fifteen thousand missionaries deployed in some fifty countries.[4]

The prominence of the Western missionary movement in recent history should not blind us to the fact that it is only a chapter in the total story of Christian missions. Other peoples had center stage in Christian evangelism before, and the expectation is that others will have it in the future. If a missionary from West Africa or Korea preaches Christ to a hill tribe in

Thailand, is this message to be dismissed because of Western cultural imperialism? The gospel is quite capable of spreading without any association with Western culture.

Criticism of missionaries is often connected with another objection: that they will destroy native cultures. When critics charge that the Christian message is invalid because illicit methods have been used to spread it, their real problem is that they think the success of a mission must mean the death of the culture it enters. It is alleged that Christianity steals from its converts their history, their identity. Though these critics will acknowledge that sometimes there are things in the indigenous cultures that should be destroyed—infanticide, murder of widows, head-hunting, ritual mutilations—they will maintain these are rare exceptions. The arrogance of Christianity, it is claimed, impoverishes humanity by extinguishing the rich insights into nature and community which those traditional cultures offer.

We have already conceded that Christian missionaries too often attacked aspects of other cultures which they had no gospel mandate to attack. The prejudiced zeal that led missionaries to ban drums from African Christian worship, for instance, was destructive. An excessive fear of the taint of "heathenism" kept many missionaries from seeing an alien culture's strengths and virtues.

The greatest threat to traditional cultures today, however, is not Christian missions. It is the combination of technology, economic development, and secularism. The concern for traditional cultures on the part of some secular Westerners is ironic, since the linchpin of these cultures is religion, and often those most critical of Christianity for undermining these cultures have no use for religion of any sort, let alone "primitive religion." While they admire these cultures from afar, they allow economic exploitation and rationalistic modes of thought to subvert and destroy them.

Often the church, coming in when other forces were already eating away a culture, provided an avenue for *preserving* the people's identity. There are many examples of this, past and present. In the nineteenth century Miles Bronson, a Baptist missionary to India, struggled to maintain the language of Assam from being obliterated by the more common Bengali.

Today he is honored by Hindu and Christian alike as the savior of the Assamese language, and so of their cultural identity.

As a present example we might take the Nishga tribe of Northwestern Canada. Converted to Anglican Christianity, the Nishga have found in the church the resources to sustain their identity through a century and a half when the Canadian government did not recognize their land rights or their cultural unity. Many of their traditional tribal structures were incorporated into their churches, and it is the church which has supported their struggle to regain their homelands and preserve their traditions.

It is not Christian missions which threaten traditional cultures so much as it is the way of life of technologically developed nations. In the Amazon basin, economic development threatens the traditional patterns of life of the tribes. In Cambodia, communist ideologies attempt to eradicate a traditional way of life in a few months. Even in a European country like Poland, the church seems to be the vehicle which preserves the people's identity and history against attempts of the present rulers to distort them.

Of course, when Christianity serves as a "bridge" in this way, there are real changes in the people's lifestyle. The result is a living culture, however, not a traditional culture preserved as a curiosity in a kind of anthropological museum implicitly rejecting *all* its religious foundations. To the charge that Christianity is no friend to traditional cultures, we may without flippancy inquire, "Compared to what?" Any traditional society which encounters modernity will be changed by that encounter, whether another faith is explicitly adopted or not. Among the many forces such societies may encounter, Christianity is one which meets them at their own deepest levels of religious conviction and helps them to preserve what is best in their culture.

Conversion

"All right," our critic may say. "Perhaps it is true that Christianity is sometimes a friend to traditional cultures, but it cannot be a friend to other religions. If it is to grow, they must weaken or die. And if they do, the religious wisdom and options in the world will be the less, and that will be a loss to humanity. Therefore, despite what else you may say, this missionary faith is out of bounds."

Why is it assumed that the more religions there are, the better? We hear often just the opposite, that there is a need for "unification" of the religions. If variety is the supreme good, however, then we ought to be seeking as many religious divisions as possible.

The desire to keep everything as it is in the world of faith is a curious one. In other areas, change and development are exalted. If there is any "natural" state of humanity's religious life, history seems to indicate it is a state of flux, of change, of encounter, of new beginnings and, yes, of death.

Why should everything be frozen as it is? Those who foresee or actively seek the end of Christianity—or of all faiths—on rationalistic grounds, are not usually considered to be enemies of human culture and wholeness. Yet surely they are more radical enemies than evangelists to the religious *status quo* of other cultures, for which some feel such reverence.

This objection does not seem so much a preference for religious variety as a distaste for conversion. It is not really the Christian mission, or a concern for traditional cultures, which is at issue. The real issue is the very idea of changing one's faith.

If all faiths are varieties of the same thing, conversion makes no sense. Why change? But on the other hand, on this same view, why be upset about conversion? If all faiths are expressions of the same reality, then the Christian faith, with its irritating ideas of truth, must be one of these expressions too.

A person who truly believed that all religions were one would maintain relationships with a particular faith, or else belong to each, one after the other. But to create an additional faith option (like Baha'i or some forms of Unitarianism) is in fact to affirm a "true faith" and to reject the others as in some sense false. Conversion, because it implies a real difference between faiths, a difference worth changing one's life for, seems to arouse hostility among those who share the presuppositions about truth that we discussed in the first chapter. Conversion threatens their dogma, which is that there is no true or false in the world of faith.

There are, however, also other sources for an uneasiness

about conversion. Some would say that faith is so inward and personal that to seek the growth of a religious body or to intrude on the sacred space of another soul is unworthy of any "high" religion.

To be sure, there is a spiritual humility in which we feel acutely how unworthy and inadequate we are if we presume to enter another person's inner life. Awareness of the complexity of our own way to belief may sometimes lead us to fear of harming someone else's soul by our ignorant blunderings.

There is certainly a healthy portion of truth in this insight. None of us is adequate to be a doctor of the soul. The most we can aspire to be is a "soul friend," and to leave the rest in the hands of God and the individual. This stance, however, hardly rules out participation in the conversion of others. Choice and transformation are both facts of human life. Apart from the ability to choose and to transform ourselves, life's richest possibilities would be closed to us. To say that everyone ought to remain in the present state is to constrict the very nature of our humanity and to offer a counsel of despair. The capacity for personal conversion is not an evil but a great good, although any particular conversion may or may not be good, depending on what we are turning from and what we are turning toward.

Certainly violence or coercion has no place in evangelism, but some would argue that *any* concern for conversion is illegitimate. "It may be all right to live your faith as best you can, and someone may be influenced by this to become a Christian," they say, "but purposely to proclaim Christ's name, to imply that others need redemption, is arrogant and intolerant."

Strangely enough, though, our ordinary human relations seem permeated with evangelism of a sort. People share with each other information about the brand of bread they eat, a way to save money, a better way of getting along with their children, the best remedy for sore throats. In all these there is the proclamation of something which is important to the person who shares it, and there is usually an implicit if not an explicit invitation for hearers to accept and act on this news.

If we are surrounded by people profoundly in need, as we are, and we choose not to share what is most life-giving and sustaining for us, this does not sound like respect for them. The opposite of outreach is not tolerance, but withdrawal, which we find in certain faiths where true salvation or true knowledge is reserved to an initiated elite. A faith which is not for all tends naturally to take on the features of something that is for the select few.

To withhold our testimony does not affirm pluralism, but subverts it, by restricting the world of choice and removing from consideration the very truth which has nourished us. It is obvious that those faiths which grow in numbers and influence are of a missionary nature. To convince the world's missionary faiths, like Islam, Christianity, and Marxism, to change would not end evangelism or establish a level *status quo* in the world of religion. They would simply be submerged in some new missionary faith or faiths, of which there are many.

The attempt to stamp out conversion and missions is a losing battle. Any groups won to such a cause will dwindle, displaced by new missionary faiths that, according to this view, must in turn be converted to give up their universal claims. The objection that a concern for conversion is excessively worldly is partly right: it is a concern for the shape and the future of our world, for the faith or faiths we wish to see prevalent in it. To remove our testimony does not assure that people will not be converted, but only that, when they are converted, it will be to something else. And the world will show the results.

I have been careful to make the case for conversion on non-Christian grounds, since the case against it is usually put so. The Christian, however, has a more important argument: a mandate from Christ for witness and discipleship on behalf of our faith. This witness must be heard and judged, not dismissed because of the sort of objections we have considered here.

"Yet after all this," our critic says, "you still expect *your* view to triumph. Everything may be fair and open, and you may respect the integrity of other people's faith, but you think they are wrong, at least more wrong than you are. No matter how valid that may be in theory, it is literally not healthy. The possible practical consequences of such fundamental conflict over truth are too terrible to contemplate. Too often in the past they have led from theory to action, to holy wars."

The critic reminds us that we live in a nuclear age. "If we cannot say that all religions are fundamentally the same, we will have to expect continual conflict. That is too dangerous. Given the hair triggers of our world, religions must be made to serve a unifying, not a divisive role. Debates over truth end in persecutions. Someone pays for a principle with a life."

What is striking about this type of objection is that its acceptance would *doom* variety and true pluralism. The search for truth becomes the first casualty of the next war, for religion is assigned a functional role to play in saving us from conflict. Yet it cannot possibly play such a role if it is not believed to be true in the very sense which the critic rules out. If the calls which are coming from Christian churches for disarmament, for example, are rooted in nothing but common sense shared by all people, then we certainly ought not to expect them to have any dramatic effect, even upon Christians. On the other hand, for those who believe that the peace imperative comes to them from the Savior of us all and is rooted in God's transcendent will, this call must exercise a life-transforming influence.

It is interesting that we have not imposed a moratorium on truth-seeking in other areas of thought while we live in the shadow of the bomb. We still seem to promote as vigorously as ever the truth of our preferred political or ideological views. There are people who are willing to brave the worst of personal consequences on behalf of an economic or a social system which they support. Human rights, too, are not generally thought to be "suspended" truths which can be put on hold because of our present perils.

The challenge of pluralism is to live with real differences. If our safety depends upon eliminating our differences, then we cannot be safe. Either our differences will endanger our lives or our homogenized security will destroy our humanity. There must be a way for us to grow more secure while still providing the freedom to differ on ultimate issues.

Our faith is as determinative of what we are as the great unchosens: race, sex, family, culture. Our faith, however, is unique because we can choose it. This should never lead us into thinking it insignificant. It represents the greatest freedom we have. In this sense God has given us dominion, allowing us to be shaped by our own commitment.

None of the objections we have considered offers a sound reason to abdicate our liberating responsibility to make this choice. None offers a sound reason to rule out the claims of Christ. It is quite literally amazing that I, one fallible and small individual, may make my own judgment about what truth, what meaning, what being there may be at the heart of the universe and my own existence. Nevertheless, it is true.

As Luther said, we must each do our own believing, as we do our own dying. Some may regard this assertion as dangerous, but we who believe in the mercy and majesty of God see it as the supreme rainbow of hope over our troubled world.

3

Jesus in Particular

I called the objections in the previous chapter "red herrings" because they amount to evasions of the central issue. We turn now to questions that are not evasions but objections precisely to Jesus. Critics who hold these objections maintain that, however attractive Jesus may be as a person, or even as a Savior, he cannot be decisive for all people. If there is such a thing as a universal truth, they say, it cannot be tied to an actual historic figure, certainly not this one.

Jesus or Christ?

The most prominent objection to Christianity in this respect has been the assertion that the Christian claim has no basis in Jesus. Many critics of Christian faith often contrast the religion *of* Jesus with the religion *about* Jesus, implying that the faith *of* Jesus was terribly distorted in the hands of Paul to become "Christological"—focused on the person of Jesus.[1]

As to why such an idea should have been "imposed" on the memory of Jesus, some scholars supposed that notions of a dying and rising god present in other Mediterranean religions had been transferred to Jesus. Jesus Christ was thus neatly divided: Jesus belonged to history; Christ was the creation of the church. Jesus, they said, was built up into the figure we find in the New Testament by an early church which wanted him to have all the selling points of other religious figures in the surrounding cultures.

If all this were true, it would eliminate the problem we are dealing with. The religion *of* Jesus would be defined as a universal message—God loves us and we ought to love each other. But there would not necessarily be any universal significance to the person of Jesus in particular. Exclusive claims for Christ would therefore rest on a mistake.

As it is, this line of thought itself rests on several mistakes. First of all, it is not as easy to separate Paul from Jesus as is sometimes assumed. The view of Christ which Paul expressed and even emphasized was not his invention, but was well established in the Christian community into which he came. If there was such distortion, it went back further than Paul and involved a great many others.

If any radical departure from the historical Jesus is located much earlier than Paul—as seems to be the only possibility—then we are coming uncomfortably close to Jesus himself. Paul, after all, wrote only some twenty-five to thirty years after Jesus' death. If a new Christological view was substituted for the memory of the real Jesus, this would have been difficult in the very earliest years after his death, when the real Jesus was fresh in memory.

Under these circumstances it would seem more reasonable to suppose that the view of Jesus that was developed *was* consistent at least in central points with the memory of the actual Jesus, or else that something very dramatic indeed happened to allow people to develop their own understandings so quickly and significantly. Perhaps it would be most reasonable to suppose both: a clear memory of Jesus and of the resurrection event.

The rather unsophisticated alternative "Jesus or Paul?" has been presented as a more rational and critical interpretation of Scripture than the traditional Christian approach. This line of thought, however, has proved to be severely wanting on its own rational and critical grounds.

The early church, for instance, was supposed to have made Jesus over under the influence of a "gnostic redeemer myth" which was common coin in their religious environment. In fact, continued study has failed to provide any evidence that such a myth existed *prior* to Christianity. Indeed, it rather seems that where such a myth arose, it did so under the influence of Christianity rather than vice versa.[2]

Critics assume that Christians' faith evolved from a low view of Jesus as a teacher and prophet into a later and mistaken high view of him as Divine Savior. But the evidence does not fit this scheme too well. Some of the highest statements about Jesus are in some of the earliest New Testament texts, whereas some of the lowest are in texts believed to have been written much later. It is not possible in New Testament study to get behind the text to a non-Christological Jesus, one not yet endowed with decisive significance for salvation.

Even if the evidence were better for the evolution model, the theory would still have difficulties. It assumes that the original message and person of Jesus were changed in the church into something they had never really been. But it would be just as consistent, or more consistent, with the evidence to say that understanding of Jesus *developed*. Perhaps some later descriptions of Jesus made explicit what was present from the beginning, as a flower blooms from a bud. The evolution of the understanding of Jesus might not have been the evolution of a fish into a bird, but the development of a plant from a seed.[3]

Whether the New Testament view of Jesus is the correct one cannot be settled simply by dating certain words and phrases. We have already noted that, even when we do this, we find that Jesus was granted very exalted status at an early date and that he was also clearly remembered as a human completely like us at a late date.

Time sequence does not tell us what is or is not true. To claim that it does is a fallacy, as though we were to take all the books about Shakespeare and assume that the best ones must have been written in 1617, the next best in 1618 and so on. Or it is as if we were to assume that the best Model T Ford was the first one off the assembly line, and the rest got progressively worse. On the contrary, sometimes it takes time, reflection, and further experience to grasp or even try to grasp the whole truth.

Bound or Boundless?

Paul was well aware of objections to Jesus' particularity in his first letter to the Corinthians when he said, ". . . but we proclaim Christ—yes, Christ nailed to the cross; and though this is a stumbling-block to Jews and folly to Greeks, yet to those who have heard his call, Jews and Greeks alike, he is the power of God and the wisdom of God" (1:23-24 NEB).

The early Christians pointed with insistence to a particular historical figure and the specific death which he suffered. In Acts 7:52 (RSV) Stephen designates Jesus, "the Righteous One whom you have now betrayed and murdered." Christians do not simply proclaim a message or a humane way of life of which Jesus is a model. Christians proclaim a *person* as one and the same with God's unique saving act.

The resistance to this claim which the early Christians encountered had largely to do with the nature of the person in question. That Jesus was a Jew was not a strong recommendation to Gentiles. That Jesus was a *crucified* Jew was not a strong recommendation to most Jews. The Christians insisted that, despite (indeed because of) this Jesus' lack of impressive credentials, he was the cornerstone of all humanity.

Today the objection is rather different. It is not so much based on a distaste for Jesus as an individual as on the fact that he is an individual at all. This is the scandal. Christianity makes a universal claim for a particular person. Many would say this is impossible in principle—that whatever truth or salvation may be present in Jesus is bound to his time and place, and certainly cannot be translated to all other times and places.

The truth Christianity proclaims is, in this view, so tied to the forms in which it is proclaimed, and those forms belong so much to one time, that this truth cannot be received in radically different ages and cultures. "What is the life of a first-century Galilean Jew to me, a person of the twentieth century?" the skeptic asks. "The Bible tells about him in Hebrew and Greek terms that are foreign to me—'Messiah,' 'Word,' 'Lord.' These might have been clear to first-century Christians, but not to me. I watch TV and take antibiotics. The words that are meaningful to me are words like 'force' or 'subconscious.'"

The questioner continues: "How can this be a universal faith and this Jesus be for all people, if we cannot understand them without first converting to another world view? Why can't Christ and the gospel be equally accessible to everyone, in every time and place? It is not fair for the gospel to be so particularly *located*. If it were somehow detachable from that particular person and that one time, it might be universal. But as it stands it is impossible."

We can begin to respond to this objection by noting the obvious fact that faith in Christ has already passed into innumerable other times and cultures. Some of these, it is true, were remade to fit the gospel, or the cultural forms the gospel was in at that time. But other cultures and ages have remained very much themselves while the gospel remained very much itself, though both developed new expressions. This adaptation can happen. It has happened and continues to happen. Indeed, one of the crucial questions faced by the worldwide church today is where to draw the line in the mingling of gospel and culture.

The Western missionary movement often went overboard in expressing Christ's judgment on other cultures. The principle it followed was not wrong—Christ does judge cultures, all cultures—but the principle was excessively applied. On the other hand, in the West, Christianity has too often accommodated to culture. This principle is not wrong either—Christ can enter any culture and in so doing affirm elements of its tradition and thought—but accommodation has often been carried so far that culture tends to hold Christ captive.

This dilemma of judgment/accommodation accounts for the tension that often exists between Christians from the so-called First and Third Worlds. We Christians in the West are anxious that the gospel keep an edge to cut against the culture in which it lives, for too often we seem to be stifling the gospel. But Christians in other parts of the world do not have the same experience. Often their native cultures have been pushed aside by Western secular influences, and they are seeking room to breathe, room for authentic Christian expressions in their own cultural forms. So, for instance, in Africa there is a new growth of Christian art and music which are African in character.

It is true that the biblical witness to Christ comes to us as something somewhat alien, but this is not new. It was alien to the two cultures in which it arose. That is why Paul calls it "a stumbling block to Jews and folly to Gentiles" (1 Corinthians 1:22). The gospel message was neither so much at home in the cultures where it was born, nor so alien to other cultures, as our questioning critic would imply.

It is true that the gospel cannot enter anywhere, be it a culture or a heart, without transforming what it enters—not just afterwards, as a result, but in the very process of reception. Every culture or person faced with Christ is faced with a need for conversion. But in no case does this mean that the culture or the person needs to be wiped out, so that a unique identity is lost.

What Christians claim as the ultimate truth is a *person*, not a proposition: Jesus of Nazareth, not a set of statements. This does not mean that statements and beliefs are not implied, and must not be defended and taught, but they stem from this particular One, who without doubt belonged to a time, a place, and a race.

Earlier our critic said that Christianity would be more plausible as a universal faith if it were abstracted from the concrete person of Jesus Christ. As a timeless truth or a "way of life," we are told, it would be much more accessible to all in every time or place. This is a serious misunderstanding. Ideas and abstract concepts, being deeply tied to languages, do not travel well. People generally do much better. Experiences of interreligious dialogue often result in close friendships between the participants, much more often than they lead to intellectual or theological resolutions of the differences. The concepts with which we work have difficulty making it through the membranes that separate cultures, but people meet across these barriers.

So perhaps it is not so much a problem as a solution that Christianity proclaims a person instead of a lesson. The Scriptures testify to this person as the focal point of God's action. In the Scriptures the first theological conclusions and implications of this person are drawn: conclusions that Christians in other cultures and times have confirmed in their own language and experience.

As the first witnesses, the scriptural voices have a unique importance, but the cultural environment from which they come does not. There is nothing, for example, to prevent an African from spontaneously producing in her or his own language a statement which expresses perfectly what is meant by the biblical confession, "Jesus is Lord." There may be a special word or words in this person's language which are proper titles to give to Jesus, even though they are not direct translations of "Lord" (which is after all a translation of *kurios*).

Christians will study the use of the word "Lord" in Scripture, as well as the whole New Testament witness to Jesus, in order to decide if this new usage is valid. But the process, the response in its own language out of the particularity of this culture to the person of Christ, is thoroughly legitimate from a Christian viewpoint. The resulting terminology is not intrinsically inferior to biblical usage.

The Bible retains a crucial priority as the common possession of all Christians and as the common source for access to the Person who judges all our expressions of faith. The notion that the Bible is adequate to perform this role must involve some belief in the Bible's inspiration or authority. The reason that this belief does not lead to a tyranny of the cultural views of biblical times is that Christians are convinced there is a living Lord and an active spirit. Scripture can witness to Christ in words, but within the words there is Someone objective and alive who is then encountered, and the whole matter no longer rests in the letter of biblical culture.

There is no more dramatic witness to this encounter than the fact that the first step of missionaries has always been to translate the Scriptures into the language of the culture to which they come, even if this means that the language itself must become written for the first time. Rather than making these people enter the cultural world of first-century Palestine, the first step is to put the testimonies to Christ into the forms, the language, of *their* indigenous culture.

This act of translation, which has been undertaken now hundreds of times, is always a staggering theological event. Translators must choose words daringly from the new language to replace words in Scripture, in fact to become words of Scripture. They do so while assuming that the languages of every culture are "sound" in that they already contain, for instance, a right word for God. This process is undertaken without questioning its validity.

The resulting translation may prove to be a good one or a bad one from an objective point of view. Though Christians seek the best one possible, they cannot wait indefinitely for a perfect version. Even an imperfect one can serve to bring the knowledge of Christ. Thus, for all their reverence for the Bible, Christians are quite profligate in translating it, compared, say, to the Koran, which has only recently and hesitantly been translated at all. This reluctance does not imply fear on the part of Islam any more than the Christian practice indicates carelessness. What it shows is the difference between the two faiths. In Islam the Koran *is* the message; in Christianity, not the Bible but Christ is the content.

We might give a further illustration of the point of this section by taking the story of a young Muslim man who grew up in an Islamic culture and knew nothing of Christianity. In studying the Koran he was intrigued by the figure mentioned briefly there, this person Jesus. He grew more and more haunted by this person until finally he sought out a Christian and learned more, finally becoming a Christian himself. For him there was no question of being culturally converted before being able to encounter Christ. Within his own native culture he met a Christ who is in fact alive and able, through the activity of the Holy Spirit, to be present in and through the slightest witness.

Undeniably there is a gap in time between Jesus and us. Christians, however, believe that the risen Christ bridges this gap. The gospel may have traveled through many cultures before it comes to some people today. But, with the Scriptures in their own language, they are free to establish their own links between Christ and their culture.

Using the first witnesses as their square and plumb line, they are under no obligation to retrace the mistakes or discoveries of other Christians in other cultures, unless they can learn from them. So, for instance, those cultures whose language does not involve some of the gender problems that ours does, and whose Scripture has from the beginning thus lacked certain sexist passages, can simply bypass certain discussions of inclusive language which are so important to us in our culture.

Today Christians are addressing themselves seriously to this direct scriptural encounter. In the Pacific islands there is talk of a "coconut theology" as Christians reflect on the images central to their culture and try to bring these into fruitful harmony with Christ. And in some parts of Asia one speaks of "water buffalo theology." Just as in the person Jesus, the universality of Christ exists always in particularity. Christ is not universal in some abstract sense but precisely in a particular way in each place and culture.

Liberating or Limiting?

One objection we have faced in this discussion was that, because Jesus was particular to a time and place, he could not be universally received as the truth in other times and places. Another objection does not focus so much upon whether Christ can be received, but on the implications or effects of that reception. The particularity of Christ is an offense in a different way. Some who receive Christ are harmed, wounded by this particularity.

The most urgent way in which this is presently put is found in the contention of some feminist thinkers that a male savior cannot save women. Certainly, it is argued, a male savior cannot save women from the syndrome of submission to male authority, since the acceptance of this Jesus would be a supreme model of exactly the domination of male authority. Christ, they say, clearly could not be the decisive event for at least half of humanity, because he is a male.[4]

Some would argue that for any woman to give herself to a male "Lord" cannot lead her to spiritual and personal wholeness, but only to a reinforcement of her oppression. Such a commitment is held to be a kind of fifth column within a woman herself, negating all her struggles toward independence and equality, for women need a feminine spiritual principle to empower and affirm them, to uphold the values of care for creation, nurture of life, love of peace.

A similar case was made earlier by black theologians, focusing on the particularity of race. The case is slightly different, since Jesus was outwardly probably not exactly what passes for "white," if not actually black. But black Christians perceived that in the West, Christ had become culturally white.

The Sunday school portraits showed a white, blue-eyed Jesus, and in response to this many blacks felt that only a black Jesus could be the savior of black people. The particularity of a white Jesus to whom black people prayed and submitted themselves was one more racist chain, binding them even in their spiritual lives to a white person in authority over them.

This perennial problem of the particularity of Jesus has erupted in our time in terms of race and sex. These are serious challenges indeed. Though there are points of similarity, however, the two cases also are different. The racist use of a "white Jesus" is so plainly a distortion of Jesus' true particularity and of the gospel that (despite the horrors of contemporary "Christian" racism) it would seem clear that Christianity is under no *obligation* to be racist. But the sexist concern is different: Jesus was in fact a Jewish male. If this be a damning fact, it cannot be escaped.

The radical feminist claim is not that the results of Christian practice *happen* to have been negative for women but rather that a male savior *necessarily* is destructive for women. Some would go so far as to say that the purpose and intrinsic reason for the existence of Christianity is to support sexism. The history of attitudes toward women in Christianity indeed ought to give us pause. There is all too much evidence of oppression of women, as there is all too much evidence of racism.

If the objection to Jesus as a male is in principle valid, it seems that other objections are equally valid. As a white person cannot understand fully all that it means to be black, or a man what it is to be a woman, or a Western woman what it means to be an Asian peasant, so it is frequently suggested that there can be no representation by anyone across such divides. A white cannot represent black interests. A man cannot act on behalf of a woman. True respect for other groups means to allow them their own voices and power. We are sometimes told that no one outside a given group can study or teach anything relating to that group; such work would be inherently biased from the start.

These points of view have been forcefully expressed through the proliferation of black theology, feminist theology, liberation theology. Each is based on the premise that, at least for the present, theology cannot be one for all people. The ruling theology is seen to be one conceived by and for comfortable white Western males, and so a need is claimed for theology that speaks now to and for blacks, women, the poor, Asians, Native Americans.

Such theologies contest the perspective from which traditional theology has viewed the central Christian message. To be sure, people's own self-interest and presuppositions have distorted their reading of the Bible and their understanding of Christ, and therefore other perspectives need to be added. But for some people this assertion raised a deeper question: Was it just faulty *perceptions*? Or was the Christian reality itself distorted at the source?

The affirmation of a "black Christ" was, at least, the assertion that black people must approach Jesus through their own experience and not superimpose a white image between themselves and the biblical Christ. It is a cry that traditional theology has distorted Jesus, bound him to one race when the humanity of Jesus is the same as that of all, including blacks. Jesus is not a brother to whites and a cousin to blacks. A "black Christ" is an antidote to the plague of racism, a way for blacks to get at the true Christ, breaking through a wall built up to keep them out.

Some went further than this. For them, to claim the blackness of Jesus was not just a shock treatment to free the biblical Christ from captivity. They argued quite explicitly that the experience of black people was the norm and rule by which Christ must be understood, as whites had made their experience the norm. Christ would be relevant *only* insofar as Christ could aid and empower them in this struggle.

Others have followed the same line of thought. If Jesus is our savior, he must speak to our need. Therefore, we will produce a new image of Jesus if necessary, one that does speak to our need. There is nothing illegitimate in this, for it is through such recoveries that the living Christ breaks forth again and again from the chains we impose.

But sometimes we may reach the point at which we decide that, if the true Jesus does not serve our struggle, so much the worse for that Jesus. We will make one who does, or else find someone or something else that will serve. The process begins out of profound faith, but it can end by dissolving Christ's lordship and refusing to allow Christ to judge our own values and standards in any way.

The logical extreme of such a view is that each of us must have a savior in our own image, to empower and liberate us. To some this may seem an attractive option. It pictures a marvelous mosaic of different religious paths for each race, sex, minority, ethnic, and interest group: goddesses for women, black saviors for blacks, dualistic cults of light and darkness for revolutionaries, mystery religions for the educated.

The beauty of this vision fades somewhat when we realize that these particularities are isolated from each other. The "god in my image" is comforting and liberating in some respects, but finally is a very small god. It corresponds to all my preferences, but has no claim on anyone else. Nor can it transform me from what I am, since it is made in my image.

One of the most vigorous black theologians has made this same point. The black Christ was indeed appropriate to black experience. But this Christ could not be appealed to as a savior from *white* racism, unless this Christ were also normative for white people, and the savior of white people.[5] Even in our separate human communities, we require an authority and a love which transcends all these communities. There is a universal truth which affirms, but also corrects, all.

We see, then, that the offense of Jesus' particularity is stronger today than ever. It is argued that this particularity attracts some who may share gender or tradition with Jesus, but repels others who lack such points in common. If God intended a universal savior for us, would not this savior be on "neutral" ground of some sort?

This particularity is also said to discriminate even among those who become Christians. If Jesus is your savior, what effect does this have on you as a woman or as an Asian, when this Jesus is a man or a Semite? Does this relationship become a model for unjust kinds of earthly authority: men over women, whites over blacks, Jews over Gentiles?

On the face of it, these objections are quite convincing. It is surprising then that the early Christians, who had already encountered arguments much like these, were so firm in rejecting them. The church resisted efforts to do away with Jesus' particularity, to transform him and the gospel into more "universal" commodities.

Jesus could simply have been made a symbol of a timeless truth. When you had grasped that truth, you could discard the symbol as you might push away a ladder by which you had climbed to a new vantage point. But Christians insisted that Christ was universal precisely *as* particular.

If God were to become as we are, to become fully human, it was necessary to become particular. If God were to share what we are, God must become an individual because we are individuals. If God were to be like us in all things as regards our humanity, Jesus must be like us in being different from everyone else. If God were to be as human as we are, Jesus must have a fingerprint as unique as each one of ours.

To put it differently, my reflection in a mirror, though precisely the same in appearance as myself, is not so much *like* me as another person is. This person may not resemble me outwardly, but is like me in the deeper fact that she or he is a free, active person. We slip easily into thinking of Jesus in terms of a humanity that is like us and a divinity which is unlike us. But purely at the human level, Jesus must be *unlike* us in order to be fully human. The uniqueness of Jesus does not end with, but must begin with, the uniqueness that belongs to each of us: that of being an individual person.

God has come as far into humanity as it is possible to come, not stopping at some weak generality. This is the Christian confession. We will certainly make a mistake if we deify the particulars: Jesus' Jewishness, Jesus' gender, Jesus' hair color, if we knew it. It is interesting that the early creeds were careful at this point to say "was made flesh" and "became *human*," indicating that the stress was not on Jesus becoming male.[6]

God became human through a person who had specific personal characteristics, as anyone must to be truly human.

The doctrine of the Trinity itself is based on avoiding the simple equation: Jesus of Nazareth equals God. On the basis of such an equation one could infer that God is male or Jewish or of a certain height, but this is not Christian theology. Furthermore, it is not sound Christian theology to suppose that such particularities are divine: that masculinity is divine, femininity is not; or being of a Semitic race is divine, while other races are not.

Yet in *having* particularity, Jesus comes closer to us in a way that goes deeper than any outward differences. Apart from this identification with us there would have been no good news. Without the full personhood that distinguished Jesus from every other person, including you and me, there would have been no Easter message, because there would have been none of the certainty that the resurrection appearances reflect: "It is this same Jesus, the same one, the one we knew before, that person like no other."

For these reasons the early church did not give in to those voices which asked, "Why this Jesus in particular, why not something in general?" To the early Christians the answer seemed clear: Because God's justice is not justice "in general." Because God did not seek to be generally human. Because our lives and our needs are not general, but specific. Because the God of Jesus is not a general God.

This particularity of Jesus seems to indicate the Christian view of human pluralism must be that our differences of race, gender, culture, and appearance *unite* us as human beings. By having these particularities, even contrasting ones, we all become full persons. In this personhood our common humanity resides. These distinctions are features of our essential human oneness before God, not gulfs across which no solid ties at all can be established.

Universal and Particular

Is it true, then, that this concretely human Jesus cannot also be of universal significance? We may first ask a simple empirical question. Is it impossible for there to be a universal vaccine for polio because it was discovered by a single person, in a particular place, and those closest to that place have the first opportunity to know of it? Obviously not. Truth usually appears in a particular place and time, but is not thereby less universal in its application.

We see that salvation from polio can be both particular and universal. The supposition that this cannot be the case in religious faith rests on a *moral* basis. It is not that it *cannot* be so, but that people feel it *ought* not to be so. This thesis rests on the assumption that people are unfairly penalized if they happen to be distant from the historical Jesus. If no such penalty is enforced, then this objection loses most of its weight. We will say more of this in the final chapter.

If we think further about the example of the polio vaccine, we recognize that the reason this particular discovery can be universal is that there is a universal human physiology. Our bodies, despite all our differences, even quite real physical differences, function in the same way and obey the same principles. One condition, then, for a particular individual to be spiritually universal would be that there exists such a thing as a universal human nature.

It is perhaps not surprising that suspicions about the universality of Christ are so common today. Our age is one that has special difficulty in defending or conceiving ideas of human nature in general. We have grown acutely aware of how much our customs and experiences differ from one group to another. We are equally aware of how much all aspects of our humanity are shaped by historical and genetic factors. We tend to think in terms of human *natures*.

This frame of mind has its effect on popular ideas of human rights. We see them not really based on a substantial conviction about a shared human nature, but rather on the negative contention that individuals ought to be free to become whatever they wish to become. What it is we have in common, besides the possibility to become many different things, is not clear. Attempts to define human nature are resented as unfair impositions of standards on people without their consent.

This position is in contrast to the concept of human rights in the Christian tradition, a tradition which arguably shaped the historical notion of human rights in the West. The Christian view of human rights grounds them in a common human nature, which comes from the hand of the Creator. The rights that come from a nature "in the image of God" are objective. So, too, are the obligations that go with it.

Objections to the particularity of Jesus may be based on the popular suspicion that there is no common humanity. The Christian confession of Christ is at the same time necessarily an affirmation of a shared humanity. Among the characteristics of this human nature are a need for meaning, an objective need for forgiveness (as opposed to a "psychological" need), and an objective need for personal and social transformation. At the intersection of these three needs there is another: the need to overcome death.

These are some of the links that bind us together, the electrical wires through which some force of grace and good could touch us all from one particular point of origin. There are different types of blood, although the chemistry and function of all human blood are basically the same. Some types of blood cannot be given to persons with another type. There is one type of person, however, the "universal donor," whose blood can be given to anyone, of any blood type. Even at this physiological level, then, the universal (that which can be given to all and heal all) is particular (it is found in some but not in all).

The Christian confession is that in Jesus we find the *particular* which is healing and saving for the whole of our common humanity. It is precisely what is different about Jesus (as the universal blood donor is different and distinct) which breaks down barriers: In Christ there is neither Jew nor Greek, male nor female, slave nor free. All our differences, apparent and real, cannot block the transfusion of divine gifts of grace which come from relationship with this single, particular Jesus.

PART II

According to the Scriptures

The One in God's Place

Up to this point we have primarily been talking of the reasons why modern people are reluctant to consider the claims of Christ. But what is it that Christians ought to claim? We will now turn to Scripture for some light on this question.

Christians have often sifted Scripture with eyes only for indications of Jesus' divinity. Most biblical studies thus focus on the titles which are given to Jesus in the Bible and whether they imply that he was God.[1] Pluralism raises a slightly different question. In what way is Christ *necessary* and decisive for all?

A person may be necessary in different ways. Apart from Johann Sebastian Bach, we would never have had *Saint Matthew Passion* or *Christmas Oratorio*. But *Saint Matthew Passion* is not necessary to us in the same way that food, or love, or meaning, or eternal life might be said to be necessary. Is Christ really *necessary* to us for meeting some of these basic needs?

The Christian affirmation that Christ is divine, God incarnate, does not *of itself* answer this straightforward question.

Someone (a Hindu, for example) might be perfectly willing to accept that Christ was yet another incarnation of God, and yet be unable to understand why this one is important to the exclusion of all others. In the world of pluralism people want to know what Christ's *significance* is for them, not what Christ's status is in general. We must look to Scripture with this particular question in mind.

Acting for God

When we turn to Jesus as we find him in Scripture, we do not find a simple figure. He is one who says "I thirst" but also "Before Abraham was, I am." He deals freely with rules that those around him (and he himself!) view as divine commandments. Yet, with sweat like drops of blood he follows the divine will which takes him to a cross. He preaches repentance, but never exhibits any himself. He studiously avoids explicitly claiming to be the Redeemer awaited by the people of Israel (at least until his fate is well sealed). Yet he behaves in the most provocatively "messianic" ways.

In what sense does this Jesus demand and assume exclusive loyalty from those he meets? He plainly expects absolute obedience and exclusive devotion from those he calls to be his disciples. His call is not a limited one. His command "Follow me" is unconditional. To those who want to hesitate or make the smallest reservations—to take even the time to finish a father's burial—Jesus appears unbending.

It seems clear from the teaching and behavior of Jesus that however *wide* his claim may be, however many people are intended to fall within its reach, there is no doubt about its depth. For those who encounter it, it is utter and complete. Dietrich Bonhoeffer summarized it by saying that when Jesus bids someone to come and follow him, he bids that person to come and die.² Jesus' claims are "universal" in this respect; those whom they touch are claimed whole—lock, stock, and barrel.

Jesus does not show any signs of making his ministry an evangelistic outreach to the whole world. His entire life and ministry take place in a few hundred square-mile area. He is painfully and dramatically concerned for his own people, the Jews. He does not take or send his little band to other lands.

It is the risen Lord who offers the Great Commission to go into all the world and make disciples of all nations. The earthly ministry of Jesus is directed to Israel.

Yet, it is also true that in the pluralism of first-century Palestine Jesus does not turn away from those of other races and faiths. He does not seem to feel his claim on them to be any less: the Samaritan woman, the Roman centurion, the Syro-Phoenecian woman. To these also he relates as one in authority, just as within Israel itself he chooses to consort with those who are thrust out of society: prostitutes, tax collectors, the maimed, and the mad. In the course of his ministry he never casts away those who are not of Israel when they come to him in need and trust.

What is involved in this deep claim that Jesus lays on those around him? Does it involve a particular kind of belief about him? Or is the claim radically "God centered" as opposed to "Jesus centered"? Can we appreciate the uncompromising character of Christ's demands and yet say that what is necessary here is not any particular relation to Jesus himself, but simply the recognition of the validity of those demands? Does Jesus present a necessary truth without himself being a necessary part of it?

Jesus is presented at times in the New Testament as a servant of God, a prophet, a spirit-filled man.[3] Peter preaches of him this way, telling "how God anointed Jesus of Nazareth with the Holy Spirit and with power; how he went about doing good and healing all that were oppressed by the devil, for God was with him" (Acts 10:38).

I have already indicated the grave difficulties present in any attempt to argue that Jesus was first viewed merely in these terms and only much later regarded as divine. Nevertheless, the sense of Jesus as an instrument of God is very deep in the New Testament, and it seems to reflect something quite distinctive about him. Jesus' claims about himself are almost always indirect: shadows of an absolute representation of God.

The prophets represented God when they delivered the word of the Lord which had been given to them. They introduced the message with a formula: "Thus says the Lord." In delivering the message, they spoke for God. But the formula made a clear separation between this message and all their other words and behavior, which were only their own, and decidedly *not* the word of the Lord. Jesus used no such formula.

It is not so much that Jesus calls himself God, as that he does not "make room" for God. This omission is all the more evident in that other Jews were careful precisely to "make room" for God. Jesus is operating in God's place, in the space reserved for God. He says that people's attitude toward him will decide God's attitude toward them (Mark 8:38; Matthew 10:33). In various ways Jesus assumes that his own actions and presence *make* the kingdom of God present: "But if it is by the finger of God that I cast out demons, then the kingdom of God has come upon you" (Luke 11:20). To encounter Jesus is to be faced with an immediate decision for or against God's reign.

The prophets before Jesus had also forced people to make decisions. They had to decide whether the word of the prophets was truly God's word, whether they were true or false prophets. But this decision was limited to a narrow message. It was somewhat like receiving a letter and trying to decide whether it is an authentic letter from the person it purports to be from. Jesus presents a different problem. He is a personal representative. He is like close friends or family members sent to a far place, with the instructions and power to do as they think best.

The stress on Jesus' sonship in the Gospel of John affirms just this point. Jesus has the credentials to act in God's name, apart from step-by-step instructions. This authority is apparent in Jesus' words and actions throughout the Gospels: in his teaching regarding the law of Moses, in his own behavior in breaking the sabbath law, in his healings. The initiative is with Jesus. This does not mean, however, that Jesus has authority *separate* from God. In John 5:19 we read Jesus' words:

> "A son can do nothing on his own;
> he does only what he sees his father doing:
> what father does, son does;
> for a father loves his son and shows him all his trade."[4]

The quite peculiar combination in Jesus of humble submission to God and unaffected exercise of high authority is based on his relationship of representation or sonship. It is striking that the response of others to Jesus which we find in the New

Testament reflects this. The firmness with which various New Testament writers reject what we might call an "angel" view of Jesus indicates their conviction that what they encountered in Jesus was not a divine being, not an intermediate being between God and humanity and not even a part of God which had been split off.[5]

This conviction also distinguishes their view from a truly mythological realm of thinking, the realm of gods and divine beings and dragons. In Jesus they encounter not a piece of God and not a heavenly messenger sent from someplace between God and earth, but the true and living God fully and truly *present in our own humanity*.

It is significant that Jesus does not suggest that his disciples or anyone else should aspire to be in this relationship to God as he is. He certainly encourages them to believe what he says, and to believe it without reservation. He encourages them to trust God unreservedly, but he does not suggest or imply that they ought to have the same confidence in their own apprehensions of God as Jesus does in his. He does not suggest that his disciples can go out to teach on their own as he does in the Sermon on the Mount, for example, saying: "You have heard it said . . . but I, John, say to you."

There is an exception to this. It has to do with Jesus' talk about the Holy Spirit or Counselor who will lead the disciples into all truth, when Jesus is no longer with them (John 16). In the power of the Spirit the disciples will be able to participate in works like Jesus' or even "greater works." But what is striking is the way in which this Spirit is linked to Jesus. It is to be recognized and tested by its witness to him and its conformity to his teaching.

Even in the face of death, Jesus stresses that his disciples should "remember me." He shows no intention to cut God's purpose free from his person—though we could say the same thing by saying that Jesus has no intention to cut himself free of God's purpose. In the face of the defeat of his own ministry, Jesus does not reverse his conviction that God is decisively with him, nor does he make any provision for some other to occupy the place that he has. Even in the post-resurrection instructions to Peter, there is never a question of "replacing" Jesus but of feeding his sheep (John 21:17).

Jesus' words and behavior, presented as an absolute representation of God's presence and will, cast a shadow. This shadow is an implicit assertion about Jesus' own relationship to God. It is not surprising that in Scripture we find a striking testimony to the special character of the relationship. The sign of this relationship can be given in a single word: *Abba*, "Dad." Scripture gives us ample indication that this was Jesus' usual form of address to God in prayer.

Today such "Dad" language immediately raises a concern over male imagery for God. This is too large a subject to take up here. However, we can note that the significance of the "Abba" language of Jesus is not to be found in gender, since male imagery for God was already common, but in *quality* of relationship. The emphasis of such language was not on gender but on closeness, familiarity, and trust.

This special form of address signified a special intimacy between Jesus and God, an intimacy the outward form of which was the way Jesus identified responses to him as responses to God's action. It is interesting that the phrase "our father" never appears on the lips of Jesus in the Gospels, with the exception of Matthew 6:9 where Jesus is teaching the disciples to pray. But Jesus speaks of "their father" or "your father" and on the other hand of "my father" a great number of times.[6] Here perhaps we have an echo of how Jesus stood apart from his disciples in his relationship to God.

We can see a further indication of this in the way in which after the resurrection those disciples began to use Jesus' *Abba* language in their own prayers. In Galatians 4:6 and Romans 8:15 we find examples of early Christian use of *Abba* language in prayer. But in both cases this language is used very explicitly by virtue of a relationship not simply between the person praying and God, but between the person and Jesus.

In Galatians Paul writes, ". . . God has sent the Spirit of his Son into our hearts, crying, 'Abba! Father!' " We pray as Jesus prayed, claiming a deep intimacy with God, by virtue of the fact that the spirit of Christ has been sent into our hearts. Through that spirit, and only through that spirit, we stand before God as Jesus did. This special relationship which Jesus expressed in the word *Abba* and which is reflected in his behavior, is unique in the sense that no one, it appears, can have it as Jesus had it—dependent upon no other mediator. Jesus reveals, or represents, God in an unconditional way. One New Testament scholar has summarized this by saying that Jesus is "a man who dares to act in God's stead."[7] The claim that is made is the shadow that falls from this Person who dares to stand where he does.

One Who Forgives

In one very striking way Jesus stands in God's place. He forgives sins. He forgives not only sins committed against him, as in the utterance from the cross, "Father, forgive them, for they know not what they do." Beyond this, he forgives sins against others, sins in general.

This is unusual and, on the face of it, totally unreasonable. It is one thing to forgive an offense of which you are the victim. It is quite another thing for a person to step from the crowd at a fatal automobile accident and to say to the driver of the car which has hit the child, "Your sins are forgiven."

Jesus is in the habit of associating with people who are quite obvious sinners, even eating with them. In doing this, Jesus significantly does not make the movement that might seem natural and admirable to us. He does not seek common ground with them by stressing the fact that he is at one with them in their sin. With the very ambiguous exception of his response to the rich young man, "Why do you call me good? No one is good but God alone" (Mark 10:18), Jesus does not avail himself of obvious opportunities to be meek and mild, humble and companionable.

For those who seek sharp differences between Jesus and Paul, here is a very notable one. Jesus never refers to himself as the "foremost of sinners," as Paul does, and never suggests in all his preaching of God's love and forgiveness that *he* has needed or been given forgiveness (see 1 Timothy 1:15).[8] Jesus' solidarity with sinners is in no way indicated to be a solidarity in sin. Many people today may regard this as a failing in Jesus, but his associates apparently did not. They seemed to find it less important that he failed to assure them of his own sinfulness than that he offered release from theirs.

In the story of the healing of the paralytic (Mark 2:1-12), Jesus says to the sick man "My son, your sins are forgiven."

Is this statement a personal action on Jesus' part, the assumption of the personal right to forgive this man's sins? Or is it the announcement of good news that Jesus knows to be so, because of absolute certainty of God's will? There is no simple answer.

What does become clear, the longer one contemplates the question and Jesus' behavior, is that there is a point at which the two become the same thing. To say that Jesus' authority does not come from his own person but rather is received from God through an intimate communion *is* in fact to say that it is Jesus' *personal* authority, for no one else has this same intimate relationship.

Putting it another way, when we say that Jesus' authority comes from the fact that he is divine, God incarnate, we affirm that the power of what he says comes as a direct announcement of *God's* will, and not just the words of a messenger. Which of these is a higher view of Jesus, and indeed whether it is possible to keep the two separate at all, is very hard to say.

Jesus' behavior seems at any rate to have caused a quite predictable reaction. He was accused of blasphemy: "God alone can forgive sins. To act as though you personally can do so, or as though you could, so to speak, commit God in the matter, is to 'make yourself God.' " Those who accused Jesus in these terms were absolutely right. The greatest insult we as human beings offer to God is to step in and act as though we are the ultimate power and our judgments the ultimate values. Interestingly, however, the forgiveness of sins does not seem to be one of the most popular ways today of playing God.

Jesus nowhere in the Gospels *claims* to heal people. He just heals them. He claims the power to forgive people only insofar as he actually goes about forgiving them and assuming that they have then been forgiven. In many respects, there is no higher assertion that Jesus could make about himself, though we note again that it is an assertion about *himself* only indirectly.

We are accustomed to the words "forgive" and "forgiveness," but if we reflect a bit we realize that we do not even now use them in the sense which Jesus did. We use the words to apply always to the offended party. We forgive debts that are owed to us. We seek forgiveness from those we have harmed. We may even have grown used to hearing a minister or priest state to us an assurance of forgiveness. In such a case we tend to interpret what we hear based on the same personal model. We have offended God, and we have asked God to forgive us and now, we are told, God does forgive us.

But Jesus' words and actions were rather different from any of these cases. Jesus forgave sins or announced forgiveness for third parties. Jesus grants forgiveness to people who may not explicitly have asked for it, and whose sins are against people he does not even know. The forgiveness that he is speaking of has an objective quality to it which is quite strange.

It may be that normally forgiveness necessarily involves seeking the forgiveness of the person we have offended. The New Testament seems to imply, however, that in a pinch you and God are sufficient; God forgives you. In this respect the "forgiveness of sins" is quite scandalous, just as much for the injustice of forgiving acts that harmed someone else as for the arrogance of playing God.

The only way in which this makes sense is for us to accept the idea that God is the primary victim of every sin. How can that be so? It is plainly not because God is more at risk from sin than people are, for we cannot do the same damage to God that we can do to each other. Furthermore, God is not liable to corruption, to the spiral of evil which engulfs those guilty of sin. But in one particular sense God *is* the primary victim of every sin. Each evil is an assault, an attack, on God's creation and God's plan for creation, and God is the only totally innocent victim.

None of us, on the other hand, is totally innocent. The effect of our sins on God may seem much less significant than their effect, say, on the person we murder. But some victims of evil acts are themselves the perpetrators of evil, or some who act sinfully are so situated in mitigating circumstances that we may be tempted to say that the act is not evil at all. God in this sense is like the infant who may be harmed—in what is an indirect but not always a lesser way—by the sins of the father against the mother or the mother against the father.

In other words, God is the universal victim. Every evil act

has God as a party to it, and it is this relationship which constitutes the objective frame of morality. Some people may not, in our view, merit treatment as human beings, based on their own qualities. Nevertheless, for us to treat them as anything but human beings, however much we may be able to justify such actions in the terms of *their* qualities or *our* compelling motives, is to sin against God, who gives us no such reason.

To have God as a third party to all our actions in this way is surely inconvenient, in that it often creates tensions between what seems "only" human and a way of life that challenges these conventions. But this same relationship of God to creation, where every shot fired and every bomb dropped has God as a victim, also upholds and confirms our *own* humanity and value, when everything else may deny it.

In this sense, being right with God is not the disembodied, private, spiritual transaction people often make it. Being right with God applies across all our actions and relationships. If in every evil and imperfect act we sin fundamentally against God, as well as any neighbor who is involved, then getting right with God is an omnibus act, which covers all these others.

It also means that God has an absolute power to forgive. It is God's place, as the one wounded by every sin, to forgive. And it is into that place that Jesus steps, offering us this gift that no one but God can give.

One Who Dies

Jesus' decision to "set his face to go to Jerusalem" is clear in Scripture, and there is no reason to doubt it. In various ways the Gospels indicate that Jesus' ministry had met rejection and hostility. The handwriting was on the wall. The decision to go to Jerusalem had to include facing the probability of death. As Jesus in his person had proclaimed the nearness of God's reign and required a response to this reign, now he would bring this claim to the center of Israel.

The response, positive or negative, which had come to him in his ministry appears to have been seen by Jesus not as an index of his failure or success, but as what we might call "self-judgment," by those responding. Now this self-judgment would be made on a more radical scale in Jerusalem. Whatever the judgment would be, Jesus appears to have been reconciled to his role.

In this sense we may venture the belief that Jesus' death, seen from the "before" side, was at the very least a decisive response to God's initiative in Jesus. It was a decisive No on the part of most of the leaders and people of Jerusalem, if not of Israel. In this sense it was the radicalized climax of Jesus' whole ministry, which by its very existence divided those who took offense at him and those who took no offense. What Jesus expected to happen as a *result* of his death, in concrete terms, for the whole of humanity, we simply do not know—and Scripture simply does not say.

From the "before" side, then, we can say that Jesus' death is decisive only as much, or every bit as much, as his life. It is not an exception to his representation of God. Whatever is to follow from this death, Jesus appears to be certain that the death itself is not a cancellation of the presence of God in him, but the perfecting—in the sense of being the final and irreversible—testimony to it.

Why should this particular death have a universal significance, as opposed to history's numberless other executions and martyrdoms? Others have died unjustly. Others have faced their death with strength and inspired those who came after them. To put the question this way reveals immediately a difference in Jesus. He decidedly does *not* suggest that his death is a model, like for instance the death of Socrates. Socrates drinks the hemlock in the spirit of his conception of the true philosopher. This is supposed to be the reasonable way to approach death, for anyone who can subdue passions to intellect. Not so with Jesus.

Nor does Jesus die in the service of a cause, as we normally use the word. He is not a leader whose death inspires and outrages his compatriots to even further devotion to their common task. All the evidence we have indicates that the "Jesus movement" for all intents and purposes evaporated at his death.

As far as we can tell, on the "before" side of the resurrection, the death of Jesus had *none* of the effects that we associate with an inspiring death. It did not inspire his followers; it left them desolate. It did not instruct them, for they had learned well enough that they could not take the place of Jesus. It did not even send them into a revolutionary or retributive rage; the emotion that would have fueled such a reaction had already been drained by Jesus' clear acceptance of his fate, almost his determination to seek it.

One aspect of this death which marks it as decisive is that it is the death of a righteous One. That is, it is not just an unjust death where a person is executed on a trumped-up charge, for behavior that does not—according to our reckoning—merit death. Nor is it the death of someone who was not so bad as to deserve killing. Rather, it was the death of a person who was *completely* righteous: a person for whom, if we may put it this way, death of *any* sort is problematic.

I said earlier that Jesus' approach to forgiveness was hard to understand unless we considered God's place as the universal victim of evil. If, as Jesus' ministry implies, he is the decisive representative of God, then it is not surprising that part of that decisive representation is to become a victim. Indeed, insofar as Jesus did apply to himself the role of the "servant of Yahweh" or the "suffering servant," he consciously adopted just this understanding of God's place.[9]

The self-judgment which occurs throughout Jesus' ministry in people's response to him reaches its extremity in the crucifixion, for here we see most decisively our sin and God's painful love, in the sinless victim of sin. This is not necessarily a universal event in the sense that every human's decision would have been to crucify Jesus; even then there were many outside the circle of disciples who did not desire Jesus' death. It is universal, however, because there is no one without sin, and there is no sin that does not wound God, as well as our neighbor.

The universality of the cross is based on the depth of Jesus' unity with God, as all aspects of Jesus' universality are. His death is not universally significant unless it is universally representative, that is, unless it validates the way in which God responds to *all* sin, and not just this particular one.

When one person in a relationship wounds the other again and again, the wounded party can simply snuff out the relationship or accept the evil and bear it. There are different ways of bearing evil. One can *allow* it, be transformed into a lesser person by it—as, for instance, the battered wife who comes to place such little value on herself that she can accept violence against herself or her children. Or one can bear it redemptively, never softening for an instant the evilness of evil, and never allowing one's suffering to become *complicity* or support in evil.

On this rough human analogy, God's path is the second. God is willing to bear the wounds of sin, but sin itself is unbearable to God. It can never corrupt or conform the divine nature into something more adaptable to sin. It can never find a lodging in that nature. So the two remain radically opposed.

Evil is repelled by the very nature of God, and those who cling to evil will be repelled as well, just as the crucifixion is the repulsion of the "righteous one" from the field of human evil. The hurts we have done to God do not stand between us—God is willing to bear those—if we will but turn around. But of course there is no way to turn around except to repent of those hurts and to seek forgiveness. There is no place to turn *to* but this cross, for here alone we see our sin piercing God's very body.

Jesus, then, is one who stands in God's place. He is unlike the prophets and other major figures of the Bible who are often quite aggressively depicted in their weakness and sinfulness. Unlike him, they are blunt instruments that God chooses to use. Their only virtue is their willingness—often reluctant—to obey God's specific call to them. When such prophets are attacked and their message rejected because of their personal failings or their lack of credentials, their advocates never claim: "These are perfect people, so listen to them." On the contrary, the defense is that they are warped wood, no doubt, but they are God's instruments to transmit a particular word to a particular time.

People made many accusations against Jesus. He was called a winebibber and a glutton. The response to these accusations is interestingly different. It is not suggested that Jesus' personal qualities are irrelevant to his mission. No energy is expended to stress the unworthiness of Jesus as the bearer of a "word of the Lord."

Instead, Jesus' person is seen to be inextricable from his message. Jesus is not a blunt instrument but the Son, the one who alone has God as his *Abba*. This person *is* a message, not just in certain staged actions (as in Jeremiah's wearing a yoke to symbolize the coming bondage of the people of Israel) but in every facet of his being. Jesus' representation of God is so deep that it extends even to acting for God.

5

The One in Our Place

So far, we have concentrated on the person of Jesus. Now we move on to ask how far and in what ways those first believers in Christ regarded him as decisive or necessary.

The most obvious fact about the believers on the "after" side of Jesus' death is that they are convinced Jesus is alive again. Without this, nothing makes sense, even in the most radically secular terms. You may think the early Christians were mistaken to believe this, but there is not the slightest doubt that they did believe it. It was not only Jesus who was alive again; so too were his promises and acts.

Those who had received his decree of forgiveness, who had accepted his authority in relation to law and tradition, who had started fresh in the power of his love—those followers wondered in the face of his death if all these were of no more value than paper money. Was the real value of all this just zero, since it turned out that Jesus had no bank and no backing upon which to draw for such wonderful currency?

The resurrection was a clear answer: Christ's promises were negotiable, good as gold. It was a Yes to Jesus' representation of God. This is good news to those who had known and trusted Jesus. Why is it good news to anyone else?

One with Us

To answer this question we need to turn back to the death of Jesus, but now seen from the "after" side. One of the most striking aspects of the scriptural evidence is the clear understanding we find there of the *scope* of Jesus' death.[1] Paul tells us that when he became a Christian he received the information that Christ "died for our sins" (1 Corinthians 15:3). Elsewhere in the New Testament we are told again and again that Christ died "for our sake," "for us all," "for the life of the world" (2 Corinthians 5:21; Romans 8:32; John 6:51). The vindication of Jesus' promises, which meant so much to those who had known Jesus, is expanded. Jesus' death was for, on behalf of, all—and the references include people who were not part of Jesus' circle, or even of his generation.

Jesus' death has not been postponed, like Lazarus's. He will not die again. He has "tasted death once for every one" (Hebrews 2:9). The resurrection does not blot out Jesus' death, but *affirms* and validates it. This is so on a personal level: it was truly Jesus' death, the only one, and it is over. It is also true on a more than personal level. And that is what we are pointing to.

The death of Jesus is affirmed as universal in scope. Jesus died *for* all. Paul writes in indignation to those Corinthians who are making a party in his name: "Was *Paul* crucified for you?" (1 Corinthians 1:13, italics added). To all people that the gospel reaches, whatever their race or nationality or religion, this assumption is applied: Christ's death was *for you*.

In the last chapter I stressed the fact that Jesus stood in God's place. What is clear from the Easter side of Jesus' death is the conviction that Jesus also stands in *our* place. There are many ways in which something can be done "for" or "on behalf of" us. It can be done *for our benefit*—to show us, to inspire us, to model for us. It can be done *instead* of our doing it. The New Testament can at times speak of Christ's death as a model, in the sense that Christians ought to share in Christ's suffering and bear a cross. But that is plainly not the main stress put on the words "for us."

On the other hand, it is also plain that Christ did not die *instead* of our dying. Christians continued to die, just as everyone else, and this reality did not dim the faith. His death was "for us," then, in some sense different from these two. We readily think of this as vicarious suffering. Jesus suffered the punishment that belongs to us, so God treats us with the mercy that belongs to Jesus.

There is truth in this statement, from the New Testament point of view, but this truth is only one way of specifying a broader reality. It is an aspect of the inclusiveness of Jesus' death as found in the assertion that Jesus stands absolutely in "our place." It is by being in our place that Jesus saves us.

But suppose we ask, "Saved from *what?*" Christ's inclusiveness is based on the belief that he partakes of our nature, the one we all share. The Bible's view of this human nature is inclusive. We do not have sinful bodies and good spirits; our nature, good and sinful, is one organic unity.

The New Testament, furthermore, assumes we all have the same disease. The disease is not only the same in all of us (though its symptoms and pains may be different) but it is shot through every part of each of us, like cancer seeded throughout our bodies. Precisely because humans are organically part of one creation and share the same nature, the sickness is shot through all that we do and are together: our families, our institutions, our societies, and our religions.

What is the sickness? It is sin, which (like cancer) might be defined as good cells run amok, missing their mark or proper function. We are not made of bad material. We are out of control, however, so that from the very mainspring of our persons flow acts, thoughts, conditions of being that are not consistent with our proper spiritual nature, any more than massive tumors are consistent with our proper physical nature.

If we ask where these alien symptoms come from, the only adequate answer is, "From ourselves." Whereas cancer may well often be caused by something outside us, for which we are not individually responsible, sin is something for which we—both as individuals and as corporate humanity—are responsible. It is a cancer whose cause in each of us is both environmental and personal.

We are desperately in need of remission, in this case the remission of sins. We need to have the past ravages of our sin healed, forgiven. That aspect of Jesus' work we have already seen. But we also need reconciliation. Otherwise the remission of sins, like remission in a disease, is only a reprieve and not a cure.

We need not think of this in an individualistic way. The need is not simply a selfish one: my personal need for reconciliation is also the need of those that I sin *against,* and the same is true for those that sin against me. This need for reconciliation has its focus in our relations with each other. The salvation that is envisioned in Scripture is always brought into focus in these terms—whether it is Isaiah's prophecy of swords being beaten into plowshares and of our very relationship to nature growing into peace or Mary's Magnificat or Jesus' Sermon on the Mount.

In a world with a legacy of sin there are structures, customs, and even ideas which are themselves twisted by sin and shape our relations. It is not necessary to wait until humanity, which made the structures, is wholly healed before doing anything to make the structures just. And yet these changes will always be fragile and incomplete because of our personal sin. It is not that either the personal or the social is more important. Again and again Scripture makes it clear that we cannot make this division.[2]

Sin is basically twofold.[3] Godlessness may take the form of pride. Thus we may deny that we are limited and sinful creatures and insist upon acting and thinking as though we were the way and the truth. We are godless because we have displaced God. On the other hand, it may take the form of self-destruction. We may deny that we are *God's* creatures, persons of worth and value bearing God's image, precious and unique. We may become subordinate to things or persons other than God, abdicate our integrity and responsibilities, bury our gifts. We give up ourselves, but not in a positive sense. We give up the self—worthy and loved—which God wants us to be. We are godless, for there is no power there to uphold our own worth and value, and we cannot uphold our worth alone. These two ways of missing the mark poison our personal and social lives.

In the world around us there are many different ways of defining the problem with humanity, and Christianity recognizes validity in many of them. For example, consider the movements that have arisen in that part of the world most influenced by Christian and Jewish thought: Marxism, psychoanalysis, modern science, feminism, capitalism. These all may have been in some respects violently critical of Christianity, but they breathe the same air. They are inconceivable in the forms they historically took without reference to Christianity and the Christian diagnosis of the human situation. They all share elements of that diagnosis: a solid regard for history, a conviction that evil is real, a deep awareness of the human capacity for cruelty and alienation.

Many may feel that the birth of at least some of these movements in the cradle of Christianity is a decided mark against the Christian faith. Let that be as it may. The point is that the Christian diagnosis *agrees* that the evils each of these movements identifies as the root of our problem are really a part of the sickness.

In fact, some of these systems may be much more acute analysts of their particular evil than Christianity has been. Like persons scarred by some particular disease, some people will grow wise about special symptoms that they know best and will trace their influence in every sphere of life, whether the symptom be racism, sexism, economic exploitation, totalitarianism. From one point of view, Christians ought to have no objection to this kind of thinking. But they *do* object, in that no one of these systems, nor all together, grasps the *whole* root of evil. For none of the solutions they propose, individually or together, meets the need.

I make this brief detour to talk about the disease because it helps us to understand the way in which Jesus is "for us." Before we can argue over the statement that there is no other name under heaven by which we may be saved, "saved" has to mean something. If we do not acknowledge that there is human solidarity, a human nature, and a human problem, then this statement will seem odd, if not empty. The only meaning that could then be given to the Christian claim would be a patchwork: Christ means money for the poor, health for the sick, power for the powerless, parents for the orphan, and so on.

The salvation that the New Testament is speaking of, however, is not a laundry list but a unified reality. It will touch on every true human need. But part of the offense of this universal Savior is that he is the answer to *too* much: not only to the problem we bring, wanting it fixed for our benefit, but also to problems we do not want to regard as such, because their pain falls on others.

The New Testament affirmation of Christ as *the* way is set against a certain background. Just as a single line simulating a road on a blank piece of paper does not really amount to a way anywhere until we have the surrounding part of the map, so the Christian affirmation makes sense in a map of human reality.

This is part of the representational work of Jesus, for the proclamation of the kingdom of God confronts our "maps" of reality with another. It is not that Jesus just arrives carrying this map. Jesus *is* the way. He is the way and also the country the way passes through. In him we see a way *through* humanity, a way which is walked by one who is fully human as we are.

The path that he cuts through our common human reality lights it up from inside. It is not only that Jesus *informs* us about God; Jesus *reveals* us to ourselves. As we are able to put ourselves on that map, we find for the first time that we are in the right place to be addressed by God. We are at home. God, who is always seeking us, can find us, for we are in the place that is truly ours.

The Inclusive Person

One writer has expressed her puzzlement about the way New Testament writers assumed they could be related to God and to each other. "Many of the things they wish to say," she notes, "take for granted the possibility of certain sorts of close relationships which are not on the face of it compatible with common sense."[4] She was thinking of the close personal relationship these Christians say they can have with Christ—a person who was killed and who, even if alive, is surely not here in the flesh—and the relationships they say they have with each other and God as a result. This certainly does fly in the face of common sense.

Yet in Paul's letters, in the Gospel of John, and in the Johannine letters, such ideas are common. Paul can write that "there is . . . no condemnation for those who are in Christ Jesus" (Romans 8:1), that "as in Adam all die, so also in Christ shall all be made alive" (1 Corinthians 15:22), and that "if anyone is in Christ, [there] is a new creation" (2 Corinthians 5:17).

The same conviction lies behind much of the New Testament talk of Christians as part of the body of Christ, who "have put on Christ."[5] The images may change, but the implications remain much the same. Consider, for instance, the well-known passage in Ephesians 2:19-22 where believers are said to be no longer strangers and sojourners but members of God's household, built upon the foundation of the apostles, "Christ Jesus himself being the cornerstone in whom the whole structure is joined together and grows into a holy temple in the Lord; in whom you also are built into it for a dwelling place of God in the Spirit."

It is hard indeed to think of stones "growing together," but the very strangeness points to the belief which is being expressed. Christians are in intimate, living communion with Christ, who is at the same time the rock on which they stand. Christ is an inclusive person, with whom all believers have a sharing like that we know in our most intimate friendships and loves.

I spoke earlier about the way in which Jesus could be said to act as God's absolute representative. We must note now that these early believers also saw him as *their* representative, humanity's representative. In the book of Hebrews (2:14-18) and elsewhere it is stressed that Jesus "shares in flesh and blood" and was made like us "in every respect." Jesus is truly human, not only in that he is physically and mentally human (and not just pretending) but in that he is what humans ought to be in God's creation.

In Jesus, what Psalm 8 says about humanity being a little lower than God is in fact true.[6] Jesus is fully one of us and is tested in every way like us. Jesus is human to the roots but also human to a height and growth that no one else has ever achieved. Jesus stands in God's place, but Jesus stands in our place, too. Jesus is the one for the many, and the calling of all others is to let him be that for them.[7]

To say that any person, let alone a dead person, let alone a dead person of another century and language and culture, can have this kind of relationship with numberless people at once does not seem sensible. But those who preached and believed the message we find in the New Testament were convinced that they had been called into just such a relationship, into the "fellowship of his Son, Jesus Christ our Lord" (1 Corinthians 1:9).

The word "fellowship" in our English New Testament sounds to us simply like a "society" or "group." But the Greek word (*koinonia*) literally means "sharing," or we might even say "participation." Those who were converted were called into the "*sharing* of his Son, Jesus Christ our Lord." It was not simply that people were encouraged to participate in the work and activities of the church. They were believed to have an organic relationship to one another already, to be nourishing or poisoning one another, as neighbors on the same small stream or cells living along a common blood vessel. Because they were "in" Christ, they were "in" each other.

If we sum up the way Christ's decisiveness was stated by believers after the resurrection, we might say that this Jesus has now become a universal person. Something unprecedented is now possible. Now one can have personal communion with a person who is inestimably more than just a person. It is possible to be with God, forgiven before God, empowered by God, all in the very act of being "in" this person.

Jesus Christ is both the source and the object of the profound religious experience of these first Christians. We saw earlier the way in which Jesus' disciples after his death and resurrection took his special *Abba* prayer language into their own prayers. But they did this with the explicit understanding that they spoke *through* their relationship with Jesus. So it is with their faith as a whole.

The power of love which they can exercise and the intimacy with God which they experience are not seen as being *like* Jesus' love or intimacy, as imitations. They are dependent on Jesus, derived from him—derived from him in a way so deep that the only expression for it is to say that it is participation in Christ, living in Christ, putting on Christ, suffering with Christ, dying with Christ, being built on Christ, growing into Christ, being of one flesh with Christ.

It is far too weak to say that Jesus had made possible a new relationship between the believer and God, as though Jesus did something and then stood aside so these two parties could get together. Certainly it was believed that Jesus had done something. But it would be equally important to say that Jesus *was* this new relationship to God and others, in that it became real for people when they were "in Christ."[8]

As Jesus stood radically in God's place and our place, those who believe are to stand in *Christ's* place. We find very strong language indeed in the New Testament about other people participating in Jesus' sonship. Jesus says to his disciples, "He who receives you receives me, and he who receives me receives him who sent me" (Matthew 10:40).[9]

The same sort of language with which Jesus describes his union with God—"thou Father, art in me, and I in thee" (John 17:21)—is also used to describe the relationship between believers and Christ. The same basic thought is behind much of Paul's theology, as when he writes; "He died on the cross in weakness, but he lives by the power of God; and we who share his weakness shall by the power of God live with him . . ." (2 Corinthians 13:4, NEB).

It is precisely as the one in our place that Jesus is able to open up to us this participation in God's transforming power. Paul likes to speak of Jesus in relation to Adam, making a contrast between the new humanity and the first humanity.[10] Adam stood in the place of us all, as the first human. Jesus stands in the place of us all in a manner which is equally inclusive but different.

We are "in" Adam involuntarily, by descent, by sharing the same created and fallen nature. We are "in Christ" by faith and the spirit. Yet there is an objectivity about Christ's work, so that just as we are involuntarily in Adam, sharing our humanity as it has come to us with sin, so too all of us are in Christ in that our own humanity comes to us with the structure of Christ's work in it. It is the humanity that God not only has made for us, but now shares with us.

One writer tells of hearing a friend say that Jesus' "human disguise" was so good that we were actually tricked into believing he was just like one of us. She blurted out in reply, "But Jesus *was* us: isn't that the whole point? Jesus is us; and it's we who aren't us, and haven't been, not since Adam and Eve."[11] This captures some of what the New Testament tells us.

We might say the New Testament conviction is that Jesus Christ is exclusive in being inclusive. This is the only *particular* one who is also *universal*, who can represent humanity and represent God. This inclusiveness was "radicalized" in the resurrection, so that now the risen Christ can literally include others, people who are *in* Christ and experience new life there.

To the New Testament writers the whole story of the Bible, which is definitely not just the private story of a particular people but the plot of God's dealing with all creation, is focused in Christ. Christ's work of representation is so inclusive that the early Christians readily speak of it in cosmic terms.

In Christ all things "hold together" (Colossians 1:17). There is one God "*from* whom are all things and for whom we exist" and one Lord Jesus Christ "*through* whom are all things and through whom we exist" (1 Corinthians 8:6, italics added). To put it simply, the relationship which the early Christians know—that *through* being "in Christ" they can be reconciled with God—is extended to the whole universe. It is *through* Christ that everything that fulfills God's purpose comes into being. So it is that these believers can say "there is salvation in no one else, for there is no other name under heaven given among [humankind] by which we must be saved" (Acts 4:12).[12]

It is in this light that we may understand the affirmation of Christ's divinity. The weakest way of putting it is to say that Christ, after the resurrection, is the same as God in being personal but more than individual. This is the core of the Christian's experience of being "in Christ." God is personal—active, relating, loving—but also transcendent, not bound by the limits of a human being. Jesus Christ, the one who in his life dared to act in God's place, is found after his death to be exactly this: the same loving and relational person known in Palestine and yet a universal and super-personal spirit.

The Gospel of Luke records the story of the two on the road

to Emmaus who in a moment of recognition found the risen Lord with them. The cry of Thomas in John 20:28, "My Lord and my God!" has this same quality of recognition, as of two profiles being more and more closely superimposed until their identity suddenly leaps into view. It gives us the startling confession which was "surprised" out of these early Christians.

It came from them without any prior attempt to figure out the metaphysical sense of it. It came because of Christ's objective presence and power in their lives. So decisive was this reality that even at the time Paul is writing, he quotes a Christian hymn which has taken God's words in Isaiah 45:23—"To me every knee shall bow, every tongue shall swear"—and applies them to Jesus: ". . . that at the name of Jesus every knee should bow . . . and every tongue confess that Jesus Christ is Lord, to the glory of God the Father" (Philippians 2:10-11).

There is a kind of symmetry to the "before" and "after" images of Jesus. The Jesus who has dared to act and stand in God's place is after the resurrection confessed by believers to stand in their place. This "after" conviction is not based only or mainly on the memory of Jesus' behavior, though that is certainly involved. It springs from new experience, in which Jesus is even more radically in God's place than was ever seen to be the case in his life.

The New Testament speaks often of Jesus being "exalted" or "vindicated" or "declared" son of God by his resurrection. Whatever else this language may mean, it surely indicates that these people themselves now know Jesus as Son of God in a way no one did prior to the resurrection. And it is in light of this that they pay homage to him, pray to him, and worship him in terms which hitherto have been reserved for God, by a people very jealous of God's "place." They are compressing into a single, explosive confession what they know of the person Jesus, what they know of the one holy God of Israel, and what they know directly of being "in Christ" after the resurrection. The three are fused in a heat which we can still feel radiating from these slim documents, a heat which bursts repeatedly into flame through Christian history.

Earlier I suggested that there are three basic human needs

beyond those of physical survival: for meaning, for forgiveness, and for transformation. All of these intersect in the prospect of death: our own death, the death of those we love, ultimately the death of all that we know. As the need of the human condition comes together in this one point, so Scripture focuses its confession of Christ around his death and resurrection.

We have seen briefly the confession of the early Christians that Christ is the decisive response to these needs. Christ meets the need for meaning by representing God "in person" and by standing in our place up to the full stature of what we are meant to be. Christ meets our need for a new past by acting in God's stead to forgive us, bearing the hurt of our sin as it falls on one in our place. Finally, Christ meets the need for transformation by opening a way to participation in the intimate relationship with God which is uniquely his own. Through that participation flow power and life. Since the one "universal person" stands in both places at once, those who are in Christ are in God, whose spirit dwells with them to make all things new.

6

One Whose Place Cannot Be Taken

The New Testament plainly asserts that something decisive and universal has happened in Christ. To read or interpret it apart from this assumption is to go against the grain. Like sawing heavy logs against the grain, such an interpretation can be attempted and, in some measure, pressed through, but it shows little understanding of the material itself.

Justice and Judgment

This brings us at last to a question that comes first in many minds. What about the eternal destiny of individuals who do not know or confess Christ as their savior?

One thing that is plain in Scripture is that God is a holy and a just God. We have become especially aware of the mandate in Scripture for *social* justice. The God of the Bible condemns economic exploitation, corruption in justice, and oppression of the poor and defenseless. In our day there is less popular enthusiasm for the notion that God might condemn *personal* unrighteousness as well, but the New Testament does not make this kind of artificial separation. It is at once more organic and more realistic in its view of evil.

God's justice is perfect, and comes to bear upon all of creation, not only structures and not only persons. Before it we are all wanting. Jesus' teaching makes this point when he warns that apart from reconciliation and mercy we will be liable to punishment to "the last penny" (Matthew 5:26). This is a much more profound principle than God's wanting to punish us just to uphold the rules in some abstract sense.

In our societies we have laws and rules which we know to be arbitrary; they were chosen to be as they are, and could well have been slightly or significantly different. Therefore, the merciful thing to do in many cases seems to be to bend the rules when they seem out of touch with true justice. As in Martin Luther King's program of civil disobedience in the struggle for black rights, it is possible to oppose the *law* out of love for justice.

When the Bible speaks of God's justice, however, it is not speaking of such an arbitrary "rule," against which one can rebel in the name of justice. If there is to be real justice in the world, real peace, then injustice and evil cannot go unchecked and unrestrained. This is not a matter of keeping rules but a case of incompatible realities: one must give way to another or they must be separated from each other.

As individuals, either we will become part of a "new heaven and a new earth"—one where God's justice and peace are the reality of life—or we will not. If we do not, we will be profoundly out of place in it. We do not fit and cannot fit. We will be cast out, as a particle of a certain electrical charge will be cast out of an electrical field with an incompatible charge.

The New Testament clearly affirms that there is a time of reckoning. The Jesus of the Gospels speaks unequivocally about a division of the sheep and the goats to eternal life and eternal fire (Matthew 25:31-46). There are also the parables of the wise and foolish maidens, the wise and wicked servants, and the talents (Matthew 24:45—25:30). In each of these parables, those who are lax in their faithfulness and who act as though there will be no reckoning find suddenly and sharply that it is too late.

These parables do not imply that we can make ourselves

righteous and so escape judgment. The point is not to become morally perfect and so be safe. It is instead the point which the writer of Hebrews makes by saying ". . . if . . . every transgression or disobedience received a just retribution, how shall we escape if we neglect such a great salvation?" (Hebrews 2:2-3). The mandate is to seek mercy and to be merciful.

Several points are to be noted about this judgment. First, in the New Testament its severity is most sharply emphasized when applied to those that *do* confess Christ, as opposed to those outside, those who have "never known" Christ. The principle is that much will be required of persons to whom much is given. Those who know the will of God and do not do it will be treated much more harshly than those who do not (Luke 12:47-48). Not all those who cry "Lord, Lord"—that is, who confess Christ—will be saved (Matthew 7:21-23).

In Luke 13:22-30, the one place in Scripture where Jesus is explicitly asked, "Will those who are saved be few?" he replies, "Strive to enter by the narrow door; for many, I tell you, will seek to enter and will not be able." He goes on to point his reply particularly to those who are around him. They will complain, "We ate and drank in your presence, and you taught in our streets."

But, Jesus says, many will come from all points of the compass to the kingdom of God, while these who were so close will be thrust out. "And behold, some are last who will be first, and some are first who will be last." Just as the Old Testament prophets again and again told the people that their "chosenness" did not give them special privileges or exemptions but called for faithfulness, so the New Testament appears to stress the special responsibility of those who confess Christ.

A second point to be made has to do with God's *will* in judgment. Jesus' mission is to seek the lost, and his parables make it clear that in this he is standing in God's place and acting as God acts. God is like the father who runs to meet his repentant prodigal son on the road, or like the mother hen who longs to gather her chicks under her wings.

God's will and purpose is mercy. The New Testament writers maintain this aspect of Jesus' message in their own treatment of judgment. So in 2 Peter 3:9 we read that God is "forbearing toward you, not wishing that any should perish, but that all should reach repentance."

Both Jesus and the early church expect a great division to come ultimately. Both are clear that God will not accept an eternal state of affairs in which injustice and evil flourish in the shade of human or divine indulgence. God's very essence is mercy and love, but God's mercy is to grasp *out of* evil and sin all of us who do not have the strength or perfect will to get out on our own—like brands from a burning fire. It is not God's mercy to ratify permanently a *status quo* in which the good purposes of creation are thwarted, and evil multiplies itself.

A third point to be made has to do with the character of judgment as *vindication*. The idea expressed in the phrase "the last shall be first" is present in much of the New Testament treatment of judgment. Judgment does not have to do so much with punishing the wicked as with vindicating the righteous. Judgment as Scripture sees it has an important dimension of exalting those who have suffered (Revelation 20:4).

What of those whom we might call the totally oppressed— the Christian martyrs, or for that matter all the people who have mysteriously disappeared in Argentina or Cambodia, El Salvador or Afghanistan? Even if the unlikely happens and these countries become perfect islands of justice and peace, what of the unfortunates lost along the way? Were they only the cannon fodder for someone else's liberation? If so, the fact of the matter is that for those people oppression and evil have won. There will never be justice for them, and the dictators and the self-satisfied evil ones of this world can claim them forever.

The New Testament proclaims that this principle is not true. Jesus expresses it in Luke's version of the Beatitudes: Blessed are the poor, the hungry, the weeping, for their reward is great in heaven (Luke 6:20-23). Many read this passage as a "quietist" one: "Don't worry about injustice in this life, for you will be rewarded in the next." That interpretation is a mistake. We as Christians ought to embody in our lives the extension and fulfillment of the concern for justice here and now. Those who inevitably are cast aside and chewed up in our twisted human attempts to achieve justice are not forgotten. God's justice does not allow them to be lost. Far from running counter to a concern for worldly justice, this belief in judgment may be the only possible guarantee for it. Without it, if those who have been sacrificed on the altar of history are truly lost, then it would seem that the only human possibility is the brutality which we see daily. Those maddened by the irredeemable injustice which has robbed them of children, wives, husbands, parents, will seek and take the only justice available to them, by committing the same horrors or worse. Only if we believe there can be justice for the "lost" of history will we be preserved from fanatical investment in new social orders which attempt somehow by their claims of perfection to redeem the loss of so many. In the dynamic of history our obsessive zeal to redeem the lost often leads us into new evil.

Jesus as Judge

In the Gospels Jesus says that those who deny him or are ashamed of him will be denied by him before God (Mark 8:38; Matthew 10:33). In Matthew 25:31-46 we have a picture of the last judgment, in which this same principle is extended. The standards by which "all nations" will be judged are set forth: the relief of the hungry, the thirsty, the imprisoned, the sick.

Jesus, as the Son of Man, tells those before the bar of judgment that "as you did it to one of the least of these my brethren, you did it to me." Here the idea of Jesus as the inclusive person, the representative of humanity, comes forth again.

There is certainly no idea in the New Testament that good works by themselves apart from faith earn eternal life, but love to others is seen as *necessarily* related to Jesus. The question "When did we see you sick or a stranger?" can be asked *both* by those who know Christ and by those who do not.

On the one hand are believers who know Christ "by acquaintance" and object that "the least" of their brothers and sisters do not look like Jesus. As our comments have already made clear, this failure to understand the sense in which Jesus has become a universal person is especially to be condemned in those who have had the opportunity to know Jesus directly.

On the other hand, those who have not known Jesus personally object that they *could not* have recognized him in their needy brothers or sisters. But this excuse falls before the fact that recognizing Jesus is not the basis upon which we are obligated to love each other. To say that we would have helped the homeless person if we had known she or he was Jesus is to condemn ourselves.

In Jesus' ministry people were forced to make a decision for or against God's presence in Jesus, and this decision was firm and clear. Here we find the final judgment presented in the same terms: Our destiny is determined by our response to the encounter with Christ.

This encounter, as Matthew 25 presents it, is no longer an encounter with Jesus "in the flesh." It comes through the word of the church's preaching, personal relationship to the risen Lord through the Holy Spirit, and relationship with our neighbors. All three of these are possible because Jesus is now a "universal" or inclusive person. As those who met Jesus in Galilee had to decide whether God was truly and definitively present in him, so now we are all objectively faced with the decision of whether Christ is present in our neighbor.

In the New Testament, then, the final judgment is not simply what happens to you after your death or at the end of time. It is just as much what side you are on *now*, which reality you belong to in the division which splits the world. On the one side are sin, death, Satan, the principalities of this world. On the other are mercy, transformation, Christ, the new heaven and earth. In this sense the whole ethical tone of the New Testament is eschatological, or oriented toward the end.

By sharing in Christ, one is already liberated from one zone into another. If we have "died with Christ" and been raised with him in faith, then because we have "put on" Christ, we must put off the old nature which belonged to our former way of life (Ephesians 4:22). The "must" in the last sentence is both instruction—we *ought* to do this in order to be consistent—and description—when we are in Christ the reality of our participation and the power of the Spirit actually exercise a magnetic force to repel that in us which is at war with God's purpose.

Judgment is in this way something like having your passport checked. Where is your citizenship? Where do you belong? It has reference indeed to what people have done. However, since the New Testament is clear that no one has done enough to escape judgment, deeds are significant not as the rule for punishment but as the sign of the reality in which you share. In the presence of Christ at the end, just as in the presence of Christ in Palestine, the division of our hearts will be clear. It will not be difficult to point to those acts in our lives which have been the outward signs of that division.

What does all this mean for those who do not believe, who do not confess Jesus as their Lord and Savior, who perhaps have never even heard the gospel preached to them or have never read a Bible? At this point we must recognize that Scripture gives us very little direct guidance. We already noted that during Jesus' ministry he did not go outside of Israel or send his disciples there.

Nowhere in Scripture is Jesus asked, nor indeed does the early church ask, "What will happen to those who never hear of Jesus Christ in this life?" The entire New Testament affirms that our relationship to Christ is decisive. It also affirms that all people are *in fact* related to Christ, by virtue of his representation of us, his standing in our place.

Toward those who have never heard the gospel, the early Christians do not appear to have begun by threatening punishment. Certainly they stressed human sin and need, but above all they felt themselves to be sharing good news and offering a privilege, the privilege of becoming "heirs," "children of God," "one body," "alive in Christ."

To the question whether any can be saved without explicitly confessing Christ, the New Testament clearly says that this is possible. Abraham was saved by faith, according to Paul (Galatians 3:6). And so, we may presume, were others in the history of Israel who believed and trusted God's promise. Paul plainly asserts that in Christ the promise of God to Abraham has been extended to non-Jews so that they too may be saved by faith, trust, and participation in Christ.

To some this raises the possibility that God might expand the covenant beyond Christ, just as God expanded it beyond Abraham. If they mean "by another instrument and *way* of salvation," the New Testament in no way suggests this. It does have a few hints, however, about the way in which Christ's work reaches out beyond the realm where it is explicitly named and confessed.

The most significant of these have to do with the other side of death. One question that does seem at least to have hovered at the edge of the New Testament witness is the question of those who died before Jesus' life. So in 1 Peter 4:6 we read of the gospel being "preached even to the dead, that though judged in the flesh like men, they might live in the spirit like God." And we read of the risen Christ going to preach to "the spirits in prison, who formerly did not obey, when God's patience waited in the days of Noah . . ." (1 Peter 3:19-20).

The New Testament regards Jesus' resurrection as a conquest of death. This is an event of cosmic dimensions, profoundly affecting even those who have already died. The resurrection has made Christ "Lord both of the dead and the living" (Romans 14:9). Jesus is the "first fruits of those that have fallen asleep" (1 Corinthians 15:20).

By bridging the chasm between the living and the dead, it appears that Jesus has made the moment of death itself *not* the decisive moment, at least for those who died before his coming. Although it does not draw out all the implications of the belief, the New Testament clearly regards Christ's lordship as cosmic. The universal person is not bound by time and space, or death.

If we place side by side all of the most exclusive claims to be found in the New Testament, we will not find that they add up to the absolute statement that no one who leaves this life without conscious faith in Christ can be saved. They certainly do not add up to that for those who lived before Christ, most notably those in Israel. And as regards those during and after Christ's life, we are basically left without a "word of the Lord."

If we are New Testament Christians, this exclusive claim is one statement we have no mandate to make. Nor, if the New Testament is a guide, should we have occasion to *want* to make it. If over the period in which the New Testament was written, in the midst of a pluralistic environment, there was no necessity to nail down this point, it would seem that we need not encourage that particular kind of jealousy for Jesus.

This in no way dilutes the urgency which the New Testament expresses, an urgency which is felt equally for sharing Christ and for remaining faithful in the expectation of his coming. Nor does it change in any way the New Testament conviction that in Jesus the decisive word has been spoken. So decisively has Jesus stood in God's place and in our place as to breach the barrier of sin and indifference that divides humanity from God and each of us from the other.

Jesus Christ is that opening, the one through whom God's redemptive grace flows, the one in whom we rise to the fullness of the image of God. In Christ God has stood in our place, and as we grow in Christ we stand in the place for which God created us. Yet, it is Christ's work that makes all this possible, and no other one can take his place.

Things Left Unsaid

Having said all this, let us ask a different question about the New Testament witness to Christ. What does it *not* claim?

Does it imply, for instance, that there is no knowledge of God which is previous to or in another place than Jesus of Nazareth? Quite the contrary: The assertion of other knowledge of God is made in the very confession of Jesus as *Christ*. This confession is based upon the messianic tradition in Israel. However much Jesus may have reworked the popular understanding of God's "anointed one," both he and the New Testament writers regard God's words to Israel as true revelations.

The fulfillment theme in the New Testament makes no sense unless it is acknowledged that God had been known before, and that Jesus fitted into that revelation even as he expanded it and radicalized it. The fact that the New Testament writers accepted the Hebrew Scriptures as theirs is not just a holdover of their Jewish identity but an affirmation that the God who is known in those Scriptures is the God who is present in Jesus.

Plainly, Israel *is* a special case in the New Testament. It is God's chosen instrument. Upon it God has lavished particular knowledge and responsibility. Nevertheless Paul, who certainly did not underestimate the specialness of Israel's relation to God, affirms that God is present in creation and can be known from it, to an extent limited by our sinfulness (Romans 1:19-20).

The ambiguity of this knowledge is indicated in Paul's speech at Athens. As his point of contact with these people who have not heard of Jesus and who are not Jews, he cites the inscription on one of their altars, "to an unknown God" (Acts 17:23). These Greeks have some knowledge of the "God who made the world and everything in it," but only so much as to be aware of the veil between this God and us. Apparently they have altars to gods who are much more specific and tangible than this "unknown God," and Paul seems to condemn these: God "does not live in temples built by hands" (NIV). Yet the knowledge is not totally worthless, for Paul builds upon it, even to the point of quoting Greek philosophy. And some believed (Acts 17:34).

In principle Jesus' teaching and the Bible as a whole agree that God *is* near at hand. God can be known in creation by those who have eyes to see. But we do not have unclouded eyes to see. It is not so much a question of where knowledge of God is available—God is present everywhere—but of *who* are able and *how* they are able to receive it.

In Paul's words, God "is not far from each one of us" (Acts 17:27). But *knowledge* of God is, as the Psalmist says, too high for us to attain (cf. Psalm 139:6). The problem is not on the sending, but on the receiving end. Nowhere in the New Testament do we find a wholesale denial that some knowledge of God is available apart from Christian faith. What *is* denied is that for humans such as we are, using our own ways of knowing, the knowledge of God in creation, however substantial it may be, can reliably work with power "unto salvation." It is not that God is not available to us; we are not available to God.

What of the evils of the human condition? Is it impossible to do anything to overcome these except in conscious dependence on Christ? Paul, before his conversion, had kept the law, and he never suggests that this obedience in itself was a bad thing. By no means! No more did Jesus suggest in any way that the rich young man who had observed the commandments from his youth had not done well (Mark 10:17-22).

The New Testament writers assume that at least a large sphere of "doing good" is common property with those outside the church. They can exhort their readers to "do good" and be "of good report" in the world—not only in ways which may be specifically Christian, such as loving enemies, but in the ways commonly accepted. Paul's concern that Christians not give scandal to their faith by their behavior makes no sense unless we assume that there are those who are not Christians who do good and with whom lax Christians can be unfavorably compared.

Good acts are possible for every person, but good acts will never be enough. What is in keeping with God's will and purpose is good, whoever does it, and for whatever reason. Paul, for instance, states that he is content to hear that the gospel of Christ is preached in its true form even when those who preach it do so out of personal motives of envy and rivalry (Philippians 1:15-18).

When Paul's rival preaches the gospel, or when the Samaritan binds up the wounds of the man who fell among robbers, something that God wants done is done. But *people* cannot be good unless they *are* what God calls them to be. The fact that a person does many things which God wants done does not make that person entirely the *person* that God wants. Depending upon the internal environment out of which the person acts, the clouds *there* may only have deepened.

Our good works may be born out of envy, pride, fear, or any of numberless combinations of motives which in truth carry us farther from our neighbor, not closer, and which nurture seeds that will eventually flower not in good acts but evil. Goodness, as a quality to possess, is beyond our unaided reach. The attempt to deny this fact only makes sin more powerful. This is the danger for those who do good works, and against which Jesus warned so harshly.

Denying that we can be "good" does not mean that we ought to regard ourselves as "bad" in the sense of being mere dirt. Jesus' representation of God demonstrates the fullness of our value to God. What is important, and also difficult for us in our fallen state, is to accept our worth as the gift that it is, the height of God's love, rather than our own achievement.

Scripture does not compel us, then, to suppose that only

Christians can overcome any of the world's evils. In fact, it indicates that, to further God's purposes, God uses even those who have no intention of "doing good." Joseph can tell his brothers, concerning their treachery to him, "As for you, you meant evil against me, but God meant it for good . . ." (Genesis 50:20). And the New Testament carries this on in its interpretation of those, from Judas to Pilate, who conspired against Jesus.

But God is also served by those who intentionally "do good" even though they are not acting out of faith. Paul says of those who are neither Jews nor Christians that "when [they] . . . do by nature what the law requires, they are a law unto themselves . . ." (Romans 2:14). In the New Testament there is no sign that good behavior on the part of those who are not Christians is an embarrassment; rather, it should be celebrated.

If Scripture recognizes that good acts and some knowledge of God are possible apart from Christ, is God's *action* specifically limited to Christ? Although God's purpose and will are everywhere present by virtue of creation, has God since then abandoned most of human history and only taken a special role in that slim red thread which is the story of the people of Israel, the coming of Jesus Christ, and the expansion of the Christian church? Is the rest of history merely a stage for this drama?

There is no doubt that Scripture confesses God to be acting decisively and specially in the history of Israel and the coming of Jesus. But nowhere is it claimed that God has withdrawn from the rest of human history. The perspective of Scripture is quite the reverse: It is humanity which has withdrawn from God and gone, like the prodigal son, into a far country; it is God who comes seeking and reconciling.

If God is to act *in* and through human history without violating its freedom and independence, then God must act historically. That means acting through particular times and places. To act equally in all places and times would be profoundly unhistorical, entering human reality in an inhuman way, like a scuba diver in a fish tank or like an angel coming and laying down the law from outside.

The positive affirmations which are made in the New Testament about what God is doing in Christ do have some implications. If God is said to act *definitively* in Christ, then God is also said, by implication, not to act elsewhere definitively. But this is not to say that God has not acted elsewhere in history, any more than the Christian affirmations deny that he was active and present in Israel's history, seeking to save.

The whole Bible testifies to the steadfastness and steadiness of God's purpose throughout history. Just as Jesus stands in God's place but is not a replacement for God, and stands in humanity's place but is not a replacement for humanity, so the history which is given to us in the Bible is representative history.

It is the focal point of God's action. It does stand in for all the rest of history—not to replace it (as though all these people might just as well not have lived) but to confirm it, to light it up from inside in the same sense that Jesus lights up our humanity from inside. "God was in Christ" does not mean "God was in Christ, fleeing all other history to be limited there." It means "God was in Christ, entering decisively into one history *so that* no history can be far from God."

Nor does this mean that the rest of world history is meaningless *until* Christians get into it. God's act, in entering real humanity and real history in Jesus, affirms and upholds the meaning of all history, even that in which the participants do not know anything about Jesus. In the perspective of some other faiths, all world history is on equal ground; equally meaningless. The New Testament confession of the decisive significance of Jesus Christ asserts the opposite: the reality and meaning of time and history.

Genesis affirms that creation is neither a mistake nor a misfortune; it is an act of love. History is the realm of human action and God's mercy. Its significance to us is not an illusion, for it matters to God. The Christian says this of all history, because of this one decisive presence of God in history.

The place which Jesus fills cannot be taken by another. This is so not only because Jesus was the first to fill it. According to Scripture the reason is more direct: Jesus *continues* to fill it.

As we have seen, this does not mean that God is *limited* to Jesus and is present nowhere else, nor does it mean that no good may be done against the forces of sin without explicit naming of Jesus. Nor does it mean that only Christian history has meaning. The New Testament is a positive book, not a negative one. It proclaims the decisive act of God, not the absence of God in the rest of the world.

Now we must turn back to the question of pluralism and ask how this decisive act of God relates to other faiths and movements in history.

PART III

Christ and Other Ways

7

Live Options

How, then, are we to respond to the question of pluralism? How should we regard other faiths? How should we understand salvation? We shall turn now to consider the major options that are discussed among Christians today.

The various theological responses to the question of pluralism can be classified into two broad types.[1] They are divided over whether Jesus Christ is the source and cause of *all* God's saving mercy and grace to humanity. Regardless of how God's benefits are disbursed to humanity—and there are plainly differences over this point—are we to regard all those benefits as flowing *through* the Universal Person, or are there separate channels? In mechanics there is such a thing as a "universal joint" which can transmit motion in every direction. Are God's saving mercies to us transmitted through some such central point, or are there separate chains of action?

Parallel Pluralism

We will deal first with those views that place Christ alongside other channels of God's action. First among these is "parallel pluralism." From this point of view, Jesus Christ is the way, the truth, and the life—for Christians. What Christians confess to occur in their relationship to Christ—revelation of God, forgiveness of sin, transformation—may really happen, but this is not the only way that these things can happen. Other faiths, it is claimed, fulfill the same functions for other people.

One of the most common forms this view takes is the affirmation that every religious faith shares a common core. Each serves to provide ultimate meaning, a moral structure, and a form of ritual or worship. For some, the only common core may be this similarity in *function*. Many others would seek to define a more substantial core of agreement between the faiths. As we noted in chapter 1, this is notoriously difficult to do.

From this point of view the exclusive language of the Bible or of Christians is not to be taken literally. It expresses a profound experience of salvation in Christ. Like all language which expresses such life-changing realities, it must be acknowledged to be in some measure poetic, operating at the edge of literal reference. It might be compared to the language of love.[2] In the transport which comes with falling in love, we speak in a special way. To say our love is like a rose is not to imply petals. To say my wife is the only woman in the world, or all the women in the world, or the most beautiful woman in the world, is language which is perfectly normal. It accurately expresses my experience. We understand what is implied but unsaid: the most beautiful woman in the world—*for me*.

Christian exclusive language is held to be of just this nature. To view it this way does not mean that Christ is unreal, nor that Christ is unworthy of the exclusive language applied by believers. But it does mean that the "love language" of other faiths merits the same respect, for it too represents life-changing glimpses of meaning and deliverance. Evangelism is therefore not in order, any more than it would be for one to "evangelize" one's husband or wife by casting aspersions on others' spouses. There is no need to dampen *our* devotion to Christ, but we must recognize there are parallel paths.

If we ask a proponent of this view why we find ourselves on one path rather than another, or why we might choose one rather than another, there is no shortage of answers. We are told that we are historically and culturally conditioned. Christianity may work for those in certain settings. Indeed, it may even be the absolute religion for whole sectors of humanity—meaning that it is so well adapted to this slice of human life that it is their normal mode of faith.[3] The same may be said of other faiths in other cultures.

We may even go further, we are told, and suppose that as cultures wax and wane and history edges on, the appropriate modes of faith may change. Such change is not surprising and ought not to be disturbing, since the underlying truth and validity of faith is not shaken. The ways in which our paths diverge from one another are due to the fact that they are *our* paths, expressions of truth for us and not of different objective truths.

If we ask about the knowledge of God, the reconciliation with God, and the redemptive transformation of creation, proponents of this theology will say that none of these take place uniquely in one religious tradition or in one historical act. The source of salvation is not to be sought in one figure, but in a universal attitude of God or a common experience which takes place below the surface of the various faiths. Knowledge of God is available equally in different religions, at least those deemed to be major. The same may be said of transformation, personal or social, including the transformation Christians call "eternal life."

The attractions of this approach are plain. All the elements which we discussed in the first chapters which lead to a suspicion of objective truth also lead to a preference for this model. This view adopts the Hindu solution to the problem of pluralism: the conviction that behind a million various faces God or reality is one. Certain veins of Western philosophy have also sought the unchanging substance beneath the changes and flux of outward forms. In such a view the outward appearance of things is largely illusion, concealing a deeper unity.

This view claims to be the Christian theology best suited to life in a pluralistic world, putting all faiths on an equal plane. It is especially attractive in societies with several strong religious communities, where toleration is a key to peaceful social life. The belief in a common core beneath the vivid variety of religious lives allows us to say that all human beings fundamentally seek the same things, even when there appear to be strong divisions and disagreements. Paradoxically, while this view seems to be the one which most fully affirms differences in faith, at the same time it tends to drain most of the significance from these differences. They are only *accidental* outward differences, shifting wave patterns on the surface of an ocean whose waters are everywhere the same.

The heart of this view is expressed in the words attributed to a Sufi mystic: "You can dig a Jesus well, or a Buddha well, or a Krishna well, but if you only dig a little in each one, you will never strike water." To reach the core you must delve deep within one tradition, and probably this is best done in your natural tradition. Full commitment is necessary for growth and for full salvation, but one makes this commitment in the knowledge that it is not objective but subjective. It is similar to marriage. You make a full commitment to one person, knowing that there are other couples, and their love is equally true.

Christians can dig the Jesus well, and they must give themselves fully to life in Christ. They are free also to share their "love language" about Christ. Yet, according to this form of pluralism, they must broaden themselves to include an additional element of faith: that whatever the appearances may be, what they know "in Christ" is the same as that which all other faiths attain in different ways.

Picture-Puzzle Pluralism

There is a second theological approach which, though superficially similar to the first, differs sharply on a basic question. This view rejects the belief that all religions are at base the same. On the contrary, it says, the more you study different faiths, the more you realize that the differences are not only apparent but real. The historical religions of the Near East (Judaism, Christianity, Islam) are radically different from the ahistorical religions of the Far East (Hinduism, Buddhism), and within these broad categories there are differences which run almost as deep.

Rather than saying that all faiths are versions of the same thing, we might say, according to this approach, that faiths represent "specializations." The different faiths have different strengths and weaknesses. They are not all the same, nor is any one better than the others on all counts. The faiths of the world are like persons. One is more musical than another, one more mystical, another the most in tune with nature, and yet another the most astute politically.

Instead of wells, which can be sunk from every location into the same underground pool, faiths may be compared to building materials for constructing God's temple. Each faith has some sturdy beams and if we may put it so, uses certain advanced building techniques, but each alone is inadequate and produces a lopsided and rickety structure. It is only as elements from each are combined and built into a *common* structure that the true temple is made.

This view also places great stress upon the historical and cultural settings of various faiths. Like the first view, it points out that the vast majority of the world's people belong to the faith into which they were born. Picture-puzzle pluralism, however, would suggest that because of these different settings, the separate faiths have developed specialized or partial views of God. Each has focused upon certain aspects of truth. The Jews and the Muslims majored in the unity and oneness of God; the Hindus in God's multiplicity and variety. Each has a piece of the puzzle that is God.

What is needed, then, in the opinion of those who hold this position, is a global theology in which the contributions of each faith could be brought to bear, the strengths of each faith mortared together into the true house of faith for all nations.[4] The weaknesses and blindness of each individual tradition could be corrected by the corresponding strengths of others. The linear, historical, and prophetic strengths of the Near Eastern faiths would be enriched by the circular, eternal, and mystical strengths of the Far Eastern faiths. The defects and abuses of "masculine" religions could be healed from the resources of "feminine" faith. Both at the individual spiritual level and at the social level, it is claimed, there would be new wholeness and not the unhealthy imbalance which each individual faith creates by its fixation on a real but partial truth.

This global theology does not have to be a rejection of the individual faiths. As each tradition gropes and grows toward fuller maturity, it seeks to supply what is lacking or slighted in its life. Each individual faith is trying to become global in the sense of encompassing all of life and providing the resources for fullness of life. In this growth, the traditions learn from each other and borrow from each other.

Some theologians who advocate this approach would see not an underlying common core in the world faiths but rather a *convergence* of these faiths.[5] They would say that when the deeply devout Buddhist and Christian meet, if they are able to get past the language and the superstructure of their traditions and spirituality, they find that the concrete nature of their faiths is similar. This is so because individual saints anticipate in their own lives the pooling of resources of the various traditions. So a Gandhi finds his Hinduism enriched by Christianity or a Thomas Merton finds his Catholicism deepened by encounter with Eastern monasticism.

At the institutional level there are occasional attempts to anticipate a global religion. The Baha'i faith is an example— one that perhaps belongs more in our first category of a common core in all religions. Another is a movement like that of the Unification Church, which understands itself as a form of Christianity much further evolved in the "maturity" of assimilating strengths from other world faiths.[6]

For the Christian this approach means that not only can Jesus be *the* way for me, but that Christians can properly claim that Christ is objectively *the* way in a unique sense. There is something in Christianity which is both objectively true and *not* present in other faiths. This is what Christianity has to contribute, its specialty. But at the same time, Christians will have to acknowledge that their own faith is neither complete nor adequate without the special contributions of other traditions. They will be expected to add to their articles of faith the additional belief that all the religions fit together like the pieces of a jigsaw puzzle into the picture of ultimate truth.

Revelation of God is present, though only partial, in every faith. Insofar as there is eternal life, individual salvation after death, this is understood to be available equally through the various partial apprehensions of God that now exist. Salvation in terms of human sin and the transformation of the world, however, can only be partial until the coming convergence is complete.

When the true temple has been built by incorporating the sturdy bits of revelation each faith contributes, says the picture-puzzle pluralist, then God will be fully known and God's power will be fully operative. What Christians call the "new heaven and new earth" waits for the full revelation of God which will come with this global theology.

One of the strengths of this view is that it does not require a homogenization of the world's faiths. It is free to allow faiths to conflict with each other, if that is what the evidence suggests. It also is free to make value judgments. It is not committed to viewing all faiths as equal in all ways but is willing to speak of better and worse, even of truth and error.

Where the first view argues that every faith is in order just as it is, this view supports change and development within each faith, as well as in a global theology. And where the first view encourages a rather isolated tolerance between faiths, this approach suggests the strongest possible motive for dialogue and interaction among religions. Instead of the static picture of a wheel with many identical spokes leading to the center, it offers a dynamic image of a road to God which is under construction and will require the best contributions of every faith to be completed.

Degree Pluralism

The approach of picture-puzzle pluralism leads almost inevitably to another option: "degree pluralism." Once it is acknowledged that the different faiths are truly distinct, that some include strengths and truths absent in others, the way is open to ask whether truth is equally dispersed among the religions. For instance, has each faith been apportioned one or two of the treasures of divine truth? Or is all necesary truth present to the fullest extent in one faith and also, though to lesser degrees, in the others?

This has been perhaps the most popular response to pluralism in Christian theology over the last century. For a considerable period the liberals in Christian theology defended and affirmed the decisiveness of Christ as representing the highest form of religion. Christ and Christianity, they said, represent the clearest revelation of God and the highest response of humanity to God. God is known in other faiths, and people seek and find God in other faiths, but never with the completeness which is in Christ. Christianity thus is like other religions, but it is the true religion in the sense that it is the best. Christ rises above the founders of other faiths not because of a different character or a different vocation or a different message but because of superior performance.

Christians can affirm that Christ is distinctive not only in having *some* truth which is not found elsewhere, but in being in every sense the fullest truth. Christ is the most direct way, the clearest truth, and the fullest life. Yet there are other ways that lead to the same point, other degrees of exactly the same truth, and other modes of participation in the same life. These are all available in every faith, though not in the degree to which they are found in Christianity.

The Christian, then, can continue to make exclusive claims for Christ, and to make them in a comprehensive way. Christ is not just the way subjectively for *me* but also objectively in principle for all. Christ embodies not just a partial unique truth, but all saving truth. However, though Christ is totally sufficient, this theology would not regard him as absolutely necessary, for in every other faith there is also sufficient knowledge of and relation to God for salvation, though these be of a lesser degree.

The Christian's beliefs remain intact, and there is even a certain objective motivation for evangelism. The motive is not to save those who would otherwise perish, for they already have salvation available in their own traditions, but to crown their faith with the fullest degree of the knowledge of God.

God's presence and action in Christ is special, but special in the sense of being exemplary. We see most clearly in Christ what God is doing always and everywhere quite apart and separate from Christ. Thus from this perspective a Christian can say:

> The claim "only in Jesus Christ" must be interpreted to mean, not that God acts to redeem only in the history of Jesus and in no other history, but that the only God who redeems any history—*although he in fact redeems every history*—is the God whose redemptive action is decisively re-presented in the word that Jesus speaks and is.[7]

Christ, in this view, is the mountain peak, no different from the surrounding hills except that it rises noticeably higher. This theological approach goes a good way toward making the Christian claims for Christ objective as opposed to subjective. Christ is not alone, but Christ is without peers. It appears to offer many of the same attractions as the first two views, while at the same time not requiring the Christian to compromise the conviction that Christ is the only full and final revelation of God. The religious task before all of us is the same. Jesus met that task in a way which is objectively the highest that humanity knows, but in every faith and in every place God is available, as God was available to Jesus. Some supporters of "degree pluralism" would go still farther and say that in principle the same possibility lies open to others, even the possibility of surpassing Jesus.

The three views that we have surveyed share certain basic presuppositions. First among these is the conviction that God does not act decisively in a particular way, but rather acts "uniformly" throughout creation. The crucial factor is the selectivity or relative degree of human response to God. This factor determines either the accidental surface characteristics of the core faith in different traditions (first option), the specialized or picture-puzzle truths and faults in the various traditions (second option), or the relative degree of truth in the traditions (third option). A particular act or revelation may be decisive for me, or for a certain number of people in one tradition. The God who is revealed in this way is the same God that others know through other revelations, but no single act of God is decisive in that it affects all people.

All of these options invest heavily in the belief that, since religion is a human phenomenon and we all are human, faith must ultimately allow itself to be reduced or filled out to a single form. It is very hard, however, to describe the convergence of the world's religions or to isolate their existing common denominator. This could be because we are not yet skillful enough, or perhaps because those religions are in direct conflict in some respects and are simply separate in others.

The fact that we all begin with a common humanity does not necessarily mean that we are all seeking to *become* the same, to transform our humanity in the same direction. When some people become capitalists and others socialists, some soldiers and others pacifists, some poets and farmers and others advertisers and executives, are we free to say that underneath it all they are all expressing or seeking the same thing? Perhaps they are—or they may be seeking quite different things.

Magnetic Particularity

Our second family of theological views of pluralism is unified by the common confession that God does work decisively for the whole world in the singular and the particular, specifically in the singular and particular event of Jesus Christ. All the divine benefits which constitute salvation and redemption, forgiveness and deliverance, flow to humanity through this event. It is the objective ground and source of our hope. It is the supreme and singular act through which God comes to us, reaches out to us, suffers for us, and bears us up.

The dividing line between these two theological families is not drawn according to *who* may receive these benefits, explicit Christians only or others as well. The question instead is where and how these benefits become God's gift to us at all. For the first family, the answer is to point to every faith tradition, every time and place, asserting that God is impartially present everywhere and does not act in any particular place. For the second, the answer is to point to one place, the place where Christ stands.

The first option in this second family we might call "magnetic particularity." Consider what happens when you take a strong magnet and stroke pieces of metal with it. The metal pieces themselves become magnetized, able to lift nails and other bits of iron. In this view, the Christ event is like the single, primordial magnet. The force field of God's love and mercy, which is all about us, in which we live and move, nevertheless did not transform us by itself, for our very structure was in opposition to it.[8] One alone aligned himself with that field, giving up the sinful structure of our fallen humanity and standing in God's place. The very God dwelt in him; the force field of God's love touched down, was "grounded" in our common humanity through him; and through this One it drew all things to itself.

This image is a rough one, but it points out certain special features of this option. The most important is its combination of an insistence upon the decisive importance of Christ for the salvation of all humanity with the affirmation that humanity may be saved within other religions. No one is saved apart from Christ; all are saved through him. Yet, in this view, they may be saved as Buddhists, or Hindus, or Muslims.

All human beings are made for God, bear a "God-shaped impression," and this latent possibility for communion with God constantly seeks fulfillment. This fulfillment becomes objectively and completely real in Jesus Christ. Because of Christ and through Christ, it is claimed that this fulfillment can become real in other faiths as well. As the original magnet magnetizes other metal, which of itself has no lifting, "saving" power, so the benefits and power of God's grace flow through many instruments, but only because of Christ. It is thus said to be possible for those who have never heard of Jesus to be "anonymous Christians."[9]

This particular approach is most common in Roman Catholic circles, and it makes use of a traditional Roman Catholic distinction between natural and supernatural grace. The potential to know God and to have that full unity with God which is redemption is in fact built into us. This natural gift of God operates to some extent as we respond to God through virtuous living and through the religious tradition in which we find ourselves, but the knowledge of God gained in this way is cloudy, the path to salvation precarious.

Through the life, death, and resurrection of Christ, God acts decisively to make what is potential, truly actual and effective. The grace that flows through Christ energizes the natural circuitry of our beings, which orients us, even unknowingly, toward God. This power flows through other religions, making them instruments of salvation when believers respond faithfully within them.

Saving knowledge of God is an inherent possibility for humans even without any special revelation. But in Christ there is an eruption of grace and power, one that magnetizes what is good in all religions and in all humans. The highest revelation of God is given in Jesus. The decisive act by which forgiveness comes to all of us takes place in Christ. There is truth and salvation present within other faith traditions precisely *because* Christ's saving grace is there, though there incognito.

Some variations of this view would hold that where Christ is not explicitly known and confessed, and so is not present by name, Christ is present as the *logos*. This Greek word for "word" is taken from the first chapter of the Gospel of John, where Christ is described as the Word of God, who was with God from the very beginning and participated in creation: "all things were made through him, and without him was not anything made . . ." (John 1:3). Christ as *logos*, as the ordering guide of creation, is seen to be present in that Godshaped impression on humanity we mentioned earlier. Through Christ's life, death, and resurrection this universal presence of Christ as the *logos* is vivified and made the channel for all the benefits that flow from the incarnation.

Christian mission, on this basis, does not mean bringing Christ to those of other traditions, for in a real and significant sense Christ has always been there. Thus, an advocate of this view can write of the "Unknown Christ of Hinduism."[10] Holding forth the visible and historical Christ does call forth all the elements of the hidden Christ in the other faith. Whether or not those in that faith actually become Christians, the Christian witness is part of the energizing of those traditions for the salvation of their believers.

Healing Particularity

The next option might be called "healing particularity." The point of the analogy of magnetism was that the power and effect of God's decisive revelation was available "at one remove," and it operated by rearranging the natural material at hand—the natural human orientation toward God. By contrast, for the present view we might take the image of a lifesaving vaccine or inoculation. Let us suppose that it is an antidote as well as a vaccine. It not only prevents the development of a fatal disease, but it also cures it when the disease has already taken hold.

The vaccine appears at a particular time and place. The saving power of this decisive event spreads out from the single point at which it began. There is no way to be saved from the affliction save by direct application of this cure. The vaccine does not somehow empower other drugs to cure the disease, but acts directly.

Not only this, but the vaccine does not correspond to any universal, natural predisposition. It may even appear to run counter to the natural wisdom of those it can help, for inoculation is done with the very agent which is causing sickness and death. However, the cure does not operate simply by fitting into a preexisting form. It is a shock to our system, even as it works through our system and restores it to health. It cannot save without conversion.

Let us take the further step of supposing that we are speaking of a disease that reaches beyond death. Our physical diseases can do no more than kill us, but sin, Christians affirm, has grimmer potential even than this. To the holder of this option, that hypothesis also means that the cure, too, may be administered after death. If this is the case, then Easter morning proclaims that what we might call "eternal death," as opposed to "eternal life," is conquered and cured for all who wish it.

The disease is from that moment no longer fatal, despite the fact that some who suffer from it have not yet been reached by the vaccine. As the range of the healing spreads, others who have not yet actually come in contact with the vaccine share in its benefits indirectly, since there is less infection.

This again is a very rough image, which is pressed only to make clear certain contrasts with the previous model. The difficulty with this analogy is its apparent implication that the difference between Christians and those of other faiths is the difference between healthy people and sick people. This distinction is false, since Christians do not profess to be perfect people, but saved sinners. The analogy would have to be shifted to allow for the fact that the symptoms and the pain of the disease are not all eradicated in this life.

I mentioned that the previous view was typical to some extent of Roman Catholicism. The present view is more characteristic of Protestants.[11] Protestants have traditionally been more suspicious of "natural religion" and have stressed the conflict between the gospel and our natural inclinations. Christ is not, in this view, such a neat "fit" with our aspirations, even our religious aspirations. It is also typical of Protestants to object to the notion of anonymous channels of grace or anonymous Christians since they regard personal faith, as opposed to communal faith, as essential.

Both approaches share the conviction that there is one decisive point of entry for God's liberating power, and that this objectively affects even those persons in places where Christ is not known. But, whereas in the previous model the power is channeled through other faith traditions, this option suggests that (while many objective benefits of Christ's work may be received by those in other faiths) the full effect waits upon direct and personal knowledge of Christ.

Whether salvation will be denied to any person ultimately, or refused by any person, is a question that cannot, on this view, be answered. God's will is that all should be saved, and we can feel confident that God will not leave any without an opportunity for this direct response. In any event, the fate of others is in God's gracious hands; *our* vocation is to witness to the gospel in word and deed.

The magnetic option affirmed the finality of the one entry point which is Jesus Christ. It also affirmed that *all* that is given in Christ can be received through the channels of other faiths. Full knowledge of God, complete salvation, and true transformation are all available without explicit reference to Christ, so long as one responds with his or her best efforts to the natual light available in any tradition.

In this view those of other faiths encounter nothing in Christianity that is higher than they have encountered in their own tradition; for what they have encountered there is the same Christ incognito. They have been drawn by the particular magnet of their tradition. In meeting Christ, they meet the lodestone or mother magnet, which is different from the others only in being the original, the source of the power.

The option of healing particularity rejects the idea that this power has been transferred or built into the structure of each and any faith. It rejects the notion of anonymous Christianity and the idea that all other faiths are crypto-Christian, only various "franchises" of the same salvation as Christians find in Christ. For Christians of this theological conviction, such an idea is neither faithful to the Christian knowledge of Christ nor respectful of other religions.

The explicit relationship to Christ is, in this view, necessary if one is to participate fully in the grace which comes "in Christ." This does not mean that one has to *understand* Christ fully or perfectly, any more than those who commit themselves to receive a healing vaccine must understand the pharmacology of its effect.

According to the magnetic option, all roads lead to the same place *because* Christ the *logos* is the engineer and builder of all the roads. For the healing option, however, there is only one road to the true and living God revealed decisively and finally in Christ. Other roads, as advertised, lead to other places. But there is always a way from these roads to the one road, and those who sincerely seek along their path will certainly have the opportunity sometime to face a fork which leads to Christ and to the God fully represented by Christ.

In this view of healing particularity, Christian mission and evangelism are not simply pointing out what is already present in other faith traditions. The Christian appeal involves a special knowledge of God and a choice, a crisis, similar to that faced by those who encountered Jesus during his ministry. To be consistent with Jesus, however, this evangelism must begin not with a threat or the demand to choose but with the statement of what has objectively been done and revealed by God. "The kingdom of God is at hand." "While we were yet sinners Christ died for us," all of us. Hear the good news of the extremity of God's love.

Imperial Particularity

Finally, we come to the view which we may call "imperial particularity." On this view Jesus Christ is not only the sole source of our reconciliation and redemption, but conscious confession of Christ in this life is the *only* way that we may hope for that redemption.

Even though it is acknowledged that God is present throughout creation, all forms of faith outside Christianity are viewed as error and falsehood. The better the apparent character of those in other faiths, the deeper the sin. The best qualities that can be found in other traditions are "magnificent vices." This outward virtue leads to self-righteousness and only draws us closer to hell. The same danger of relying on virtue exists for Christians themselves, since the only way of salvation is trust in the atoning death of Christ.

This view plainly affirms the objective character of God's act in Christ, but it is not understood to have already affected *all* persons as is the case in different ways in the two previous options. Only through faith do you enter the sphere of salvation; only then God's act becomes effective for you. Evangelism has a burning urgency to seek conversion of all the lost who stand in the shadow of death. Apart from conversion, they have no hope.

It need not be denied in this view that God offers grace to all people in every situation. All humanity is without excuse. This means that God has extended a hand to humanity which sin inevitably pushes aside. God's self-revelation is a witness that only serves to condemn us, since we reject it. God's merciful will toward all creation is never in question.

The focus instead is on God's justice and grace *after* the universal rejection of God's fundamental gift to us in creation. After this rejection it has been God's mercy to go above and beyond what justice demands and to bear the penalty of our sin. God's objective redemptive act, however, has not been automatic for any person, has not canceled in any way human freedom and historical existence. It is offered without coercion for those who will believe, offered through historical and human agencies.

God is like the employer in Jesus' parable who hired workers for only the last hour of the day and paid them the same as those who worked all day. God is under no obligation to satisfy the sensibilities of sinners like ourselves: "Am I not allowed to do what I choose with what belongs to me? Or do you begrudge my generosity?" (Matthew 20:15).

On this view, revelation of God's character, forgiveness of sins, and true transformation are all present only within the community of those who have found and accepted Christ. There is no question of a "hidden Christ" in other traditions. Christ and Christ's benefits are present only where his name is named. This does not mean that God is absent from the rest of human life, but that presence is either through the witness given by the natural creation *or* the movement of the

Holy Spirit, which guides those on their way to faith. Neither, however, is sufficient to save.

If some people object that this means only a few will be saved, the response will be that this matter is not settled by arithmetic. God's rule of the world is just, and justice remains the same whether the majority defies it or not. It is a fact that only some are fed in our world, while many go hungry. God has provided all that is needed for each to eat, but we have spurned this grace. It is the same with salvation.

Even within this view, however, there are certain elements which almost inevitably broaden the path of salvation. The first is the question of those who lived prior to the life of Jesus, especially in Israel. The second is the question of those who never become capable of faith: those who die as infants, the severely retarded. A third has to do with those who have never been reached in any form by the gospel of Christ, those whom Roman Catholic theology has designated the "invincibly ignorant." Will they never be offered the over-and-above grace of Christ? Many who hold this view would not definitely say no.

At this point, those who hold this theology want to beware of raising false hopes. To say that people will certainly have a choice after death could weaken our resolve to witness to them, and so in fact place their souls in greater danger. Yet in extremity, those who hold to this theology know that this judgment is not theirs to make. They can simply say of non-Christians, "Our only hope is grace, and that on the basis of what God . . . did in Christ at the cross. And this is their only hope too."[12] The very respect for God's freedom which says that we sinners cannot complain of God's free grace to some, when all deserve condemnation, also says that God cannot be limited or prevented from giving special grace outside the ordinary channels.

These, then, are the primary live options before the Christian community as it reflects on the reality of other faiths around it. In the next chapter I will offer a few of my own reflections on the fundamental issues which these various options raise.

Is Christ the Only Way?

Christians can and should continue to confess Jesus Christ as the way, the truth, and the life. They should, because the heart of the biblical witness and of Christian experience beats with this confession. They can, because none of the objections against truth in the realm of faith, none of the attempts to rule out this faith in Christ on the grounds of its "oppressive" consequences stands up to reason. If we are to rule out Christian faith on such grounds, we must rule out most of what has any significance in human conviction.

The Way: Universal and Particular

Christians confess Christ as *the* way. This means not merely that Christ *opens* the way to salvation but that Christ *is* the way, because being "in Christ" enables us to travel this way of salvation to its ultimate conclusion. The Christian way leads only to one end, and it finally must go through or be "in" Christ, as a road must go through a tunnel which is the only passage in a mountain. But the paths leading to this end do not *start* from only one place.

As you look at a map, you may see a destination which itself is reached only by one way. From all the various points on that map, however, you would follow quite different paths to come to that one way and so reach that destination. Over the last necessary stage, these paths become the same. Without that ultimate one way it would not be possible to get to *this* destination at all, from any of those points.

Contrary to the magnetic model, the Christ event has not taken over all other roads and made them fit only to travel toward Christ. One can still travel them to other destinations. It is not as though by following your compass faithfully north from St. Louis toward Chicago, and sticking virtuously with good conscience to this aim, you would find that Christ has "magnetized" your compass so that you end up in Dallas.

The Christ event has objectively changed and affected all human paths, but not by making them all necessarily lead to the same place. They have all been changed because now they all objectively have a new possible destination in Christ. People on all these paths are, by their seeking and loving, aiming toward this destination or some other. Until there is some way made from the foot of an Andean mountain to a village that lies at its crest, the road that lies at my front door does not lead to that village. And when a way has been broken through, all other roads become, by that fact, a new, additional kind of way.

It is in this sense that it seems to me Christians regard Christ as *the* way. God, who was "far off" has come near: a way has been opened for reconciliation and communion. On our journey to meet and respond to God's movement toward us, we must pass this bridge. But as Jesus said, many will come from all points of the compass to share in the feast, starting from numberless places and coming by countless routes.

To put it differently, *the* way would not be as it is, were there not the barriers of sin and death between us and God. Christ is the way through these to reconciliation with God, with all which that means in terms of transformation into new creatures. In Christ's ministry we saw how forgiveness broke through to outcasts and sinners. Christians believe that in Christ's life, death, and resurrection this breakthrough is made permanent, so that the power of sin and death are overcome with forgiveness and life.

Through this particular One who absolutely represents God and absolutely represents us, a hole has been pushed through the sky and time itself. And through this opening the light and grace of God stream, like sunshine after rain. They touch and nurture everything to some extent, regardless of whether there is any idea of how or when this rift in the clouds of sin came to be. Christ's breakthrough is a way, for it can be declined. It is *the* way, for there is no other way to full reconciliation with God.

One modern writer has argued we cannot say "that all who are saved are saved by Jesus of Nazareth."[1] In one very limited sense his argument is completely true. Those who are saved from drowning by a lifeguard, or those who are saved from sweatshop labor by legislation, or those who are saved from a mental breakdown by astrology are not saved by Christ (though Christians would want to say that the universal effect of Christ may have a part even in such events).

But the Christian affirmation is that all who come to what Christians mean by salvation—reconciliation with the personal, living God who made us and loves us—*do* come by Christ. Christ is the particular way to whom all who would reach this particular destination from their many starting points come, and in whom they are carried across the part of the road none of us may pass alone.

The Truth: Defining Without Confining

Christians believe Christ to be the decisive self-revelation of God. As such, Christ meets the ultimate human need for meaning and truth. The definitive word which is given in the gospel is that "God is Christlike and in God there is no un-Christlikeness at all."[2] One thing that it means to be a Christian is to cling to this in all circumstances as the final word. Martin Luther put it perfectly: "I have no God whether in heaven or in earth, and I know of none, outside the flesh that lies in the bosom of the Virgin Mary. For elsewhere God is utterly incomprehensible, but comprehensible in the flesh of Christ alone."[3]

What does this mean in regard to truth outside of Christ?

To say that God is decisively defined by Christ does not mean that God is *exhausted* in Christ or totally confined to Christ. God was revealed through the prophets to Israel. God is present to every seeking heart, to all who do not know the name of Christ but turn within their own traditions toward what they know of God, crying "I believe, help thou my unbelief."

Is there, then, knowledge of God in other faith traditions? If we were to say No, we would be saying in effect that apart from God's initiative in Christ, God has not been always seeking the lost, always reaching out to humanity. God *has* sought to be known. If, as Christians believe, Christ represents the clearest knowledge of God, then we must say that this God is not known save in the most fragmentary way in most other faiths. Yet these fragments are true fragments.

The Christian will want to affirm this judgment and at the same time recognize that it is made from outside these faiths. It is a Christian judgment. From within those faiths, what we see as fragments are part of a whole, which is entirely distinct from the Christian confession. We have no desire to suggest that these faiths are just second-class ways of being Christian, but from our own faith perspective we can affirm that there is knowledge of God present in these faiths such that it can place persons on the path toward the knowledge which is in Christ. To say that the *same* knowledge is present in the different faiths is not only to fly in the face of the evidence, but to deny the integrity of each.

All truth comes from God and is of God. This axiom applies to truths of nature, of pure reason like mathematics, of medicine, of art. Not all of these, indeed almost none of these, are given in Christ. In Christ we get to know *God*, God's will and nature, above all God's will toward *us*. We do not get to know all of what God *knows* or all that God *does*.

As Christians we ought to rejoice at all truth as part of the wider scope of God. We stand in awe before the universe as astronomers uncover it for us or physicists sketch it. Since we believe that Christ reflects the very image of God, the God whose purpose and hand are the source of all this, we feel that these truths cannot be apart from Christ. Nevertheless, they are perfectly accessible to those who are apart from Christ.

Important though such truth is, to Christians it is in a sense "background," since it does not tell us the central thing we objectively need: the truth that has to do with us, our purpose, our sin, and our deliverance. To Christians it seems that the secular faiths in our pluralistic world try to take what they believe to be objective truths about the world, whether in biology or physics or psychology, and transpose them into this truth that we so desperately need, the truth about ourselves. Even on a purely rational basis, we may argue that this can hardly work.

It is a "category mistake" to suppose, for instance, that close biological study of human DNA will provide an answer to the meaning of life. This is to confuse answers of functional fact with answers of ultimate purpose and value. What we are biologically programmed to do or predisposed to do is a fact, but it cannot tell us in what way to change this programming, as the capacity for such change arises. What we are does not tell us what we ought to be.

The truth about us is not "out there" in factual information about other parts of the universe. That is why the Bible is not primarily a book conveying that sort of information. We may thank God that even in our frail condition we can discover much of that ourselves. Furthermore, much that we discover does indeed lead us to discern the boundaries, so to speak, within which the answer to our need must lie.

But this answer itself cannot be discovered like a dinosaur bone or a new element. As we have already said, Christ not only decisively defines God, but decisively defines humanity. Christ does not *exhaust* what it means to be human, but Christ reveals the depth of what humanity is by nature and destiny, both the true nature of our need and the full dimensions of our hope. This is what we need to know about ourselves.

Not all truth is given in Christ but, as the New Testament says, all truth hangs together in Christ. Beyond our limited horizon all lines of truth converge toward Christ, simply because Christ reveals the one from whom all things come. A prominent Christian missionary has said that to claim finality for Jesus Christ is not to assert that the majority will some day be Christians or that all others will be damned. It is to claim that commitment to him is the way in which we can become truly aligned to the ultimate end for which all things were made.[4] It is *this* that Christ reveals. It is in this sense that Christ is *the* truth.

We can summarize the Christian claim in Christ in a few points. To know Christ is to know God in a way not available in any other revelation. It is to know all that we *need* to know of God. The whole event of Christ defines our human nature: No one who reaches the true goal of human existence will have done so without approximating the humanity of Jesus. This means that history itself finally is judged according to the measure which is given in Jesus Christ. These truths are not only validated but made real and available to all persons by the unique aliveness of the person of Christ.[5] Christ is, in short, the living measure to which no other gauge is adequate.

The Life: Help and Hope

In the Gospel of John, Jesus says, "I came that they may have life, and have it abundantly" (John 10:10). On the face of it, this declaration is even more perplexing than a confession of Christ as the way or the truth. Life is after all a quite concrete and universal reality. It would be ridiculous to suppose that only Christians are alive. It is easy, then, to say quickly that what Christians are talking about is a life after death, eternal life.

But what the New Testament says of life in Christ cannot be so narrowly limited. On all sides evil threatens even our concrete biological life: nuclear weapons, toxic pollution, race hatreds, starvation, wars, and crime. Is the simple preservation of life or simple justice totally unrelated to the life which comes in Christ? On biblical grounds we could hardly say so. A good deal of the New Testament account of Jesus is devoted to his concern for concrete human life, both in physical healing and in the condemnation of injustice.

The human need is not only for meaning and truth, or for forgiveness, but for transformation, "new life." This fact is plain at the most concrete and tangible level, where the world's people need the new life of enough to eat, the new life of freedom from sudden death and imprisonment, the new life of work and wage to support a family, the new life of dignity and freedom of expression. Death and sin are the powers that rule our world, the shadows in which life is lived. It is from oppression by these powers that we need to be liberated and transformed. Christ came to restore life, in its simplest as well as its fullest sense. Salvation does not mean *only* deliverance from sickness and oppression but it does not mean less.

What does all this mean in terms of pluralism? Whenever someone does a good deed, does he or she automatically become a Christian, since it is God's will that all people have life? No. However, as Matthew 25 makes clear, whenever good is done or evil resisted, Christ is served, and the grace of Christ is active. Wherever life has been rescued from sin or death in any time, God has upheld that act in all good pleasure. The purpose and end of all creation, the transformation that Christians see begun and accomplished in Christ, is furthered by every loving and just act.

Does this mean that people can participate in building God's reign, without being Christians, without seeking or finding Christian salvation? Yes. We can never say that this building is done alone or without God's grace, but we should freely acknowledge that it is done. The visions of justice and peace and joy which are pursued by those in other faith traditions at certain points correspond to the "new heaven and new earth" that Christians expect.

What, then, is the unique life which Christians confess comes in Christ alone? It is not only personal immortality, in communion and unity with God. It includes this, which already separates it from many other faiths, but it is most distinctively a personal relationship between the Christian and the living Christ. It is a living hope, which experiences the power of Christ in *all* life-giving processes, vivifying them and confirming them.

To appreciate this truth, we need to reflect on life as we know it. Whenever humans struggle to make life livable, to resist evil and limit injustice, they behave in a fundamentally ambiguous way. Sometimes the results are tragic: it is no news that some of the most horrible of history's pages have been written by those who were sincerely trying to do good by rooting out evil. Sometimes circumstance twists results directly counter to our good intent. Sin corrupts even the highest triumphs of good.

When we achieve our best approximation of justice or good, we are still aware that it is temporary, liable to be swept away in a new storm of evil. In an ultimate sense such gains are only postponements: postponements of new ills, postponements of death itself. All our accomplishments suffer from this knowledge that they are sand castles before a rising tide.

Christians believe, however, that Christ is both the sign and the source of true transformation. On the one hand, this means that all the movements toward justice and peace will finally be permanently realized and on the other hand, that no single act in this direction will be lost or futile. The light of Easter morning streams both backward and forward in time, giving every good act a new significance.

Whatever some act may objectively accomplish in its own moment and place, it now is energized by the Christ event as a sign, a foretaste of the true end of history.[6] Hope is a Christian virtue for this reason; it is not a dream about what might be, but a firm hold on what has been done in Christ. So Christians have a special perspective on all the forces working to uphold life in our world, and a special resource for daily devotion to them, even against all realistic expectations.

There is special power and grace that comes from being consciously "in Christ." This relationship is not only focused on hope for transformation of the world; above all it is focused on the transformation of self, for this is finally inseparable from what the New Testament calls life or eternal life. The reign of God cannot come while we refuse to live under it, or while we remain alien to its climate and atmosphere. Many of the Puritan devotionals speak of learning to "love holiness." What they so indicate is that our very being must become new. We do need not only to bridle and restrain our emotions and desires, forcing them to serve good ends rather than bad; we must grow new desires, which rejoice in justice and holiness themselves. Our loves need to be transformed, and Christians testify that this change comes "in Christ."

Life thus has many levels and is threatened in many ways. At many of these levels Christians can work wholeheartedly with others. When some Muslims and Jews and Christians and Hindus band together in an English community to overcome the riots and hostility that exist among their various communities because of ethnic and religious differences, this is a saving act. Likewise, when Hindus, Christians, and Muslims work together in an Indian village to provide a well with clean drinking water and so deliver the village from sickness and death, this too is a saving act. They are overcoming evil through love. And as Christians we may say that, wherever evil is overcome through love, it is also by grace.

In these concrete ways, all in these groups participate together in overcoming evil. Each still understands it in terms of his or her own faith. And these saving acts themselves figure in understandings of ultimate salvation which are different. Clean water, for instance, is not the final and definitive purpose and end of existence in any of these faiths. In addition to salvation from evil through love, there is also salvation from sin through faith, which Christians view as the true fullness of life: communion with God.

We cannot say that these two levels of salvation simply exist in different worlds. We can find areas of common struggle and must always seek to expand these. Nevertheless, such struggles, and the very ideas of what must be struggled against or for, are themselves shaped by the convictions about final salvation. For many of the urgent evils that confront us, we of various faiths can find sufficient ground to act together, but we will never be able to pursue mere human justice and peace by putting other kinds of salvation on "hold." Justice and peace themselves have meaning and worth only as we are gripped by some revelation of life in its truth and fullness.

Christians and Other Faiths

What does all this imply about other religious faiths? The first thing that it implies is that they are to be regarded with utmost seriousness and respect. They are not to be made or remade into anonymous forms of Christianity. Some maintain that every faith works to reach the same salvation, because Christ really works in a hidden way through them all. To me this seems more imperialistic, not less, than to say simply that you cannot come ultimately to the God who is definitively revealed in Christ by any way but Christ.

Christians do not regard other faiths as wrong in the sense

that they try to be Christian and fail. The point is that other faiths are not trying to be Christian. They are not seeking reconciliation and communion with the personal God who is one with Christ. We must say of other faiths that they succeed in being what they intend to be. The Buddhist is not seeking heaven and just calling it *nirvana*. The Buddhist is seeking *nirvana*, a state that is wholly different from heaven, incompatible with what Christians know of God's personal nature and of the value of created personhood. The faiths of the world are decidedly not all different forms of the same thing.

Christians do not mean that other faiths are wrong in the sense that they produce nothing good or beautiful. In both respects they may equal or surpass Christianity. This may even be so in terms of what we might call spiritual technique. Christians mean, or ought to mean, that these other faiths are wrong as the framework of ultimate belief. This is an objective claim about the nature of the cosmos and God's presence in it. Christians also mean that insofar as these faiths do not take the true measure of God and humanity, they cannot alone solve the human problem.

This sounds like an enormous claim, and it is. But in one sense it is simply a truism. None of these faiths is *trying* to solve the human problem as Christianity understands it. Each understands it differently. Much of the argument about which religion or religions "work" is hopelessly misguided, for almost all faiths work in some way. The question is "For what?" The world of faith is not like a single lock with many keys, only one of which fits. It is rather like many locks, with many keys that open them. The question is, what does each lock open, and to what does it belong?

Is there salvation in all religions? If salvation is an experience of mystical union with "the One," then Hinduism can save. If it is an experience of illumination and release from all desire, including the desire for good, then Buddhism can save. If it is faithfulness to one's ancestors, then Shintoism can save. If it is revolution against a privileged class and for state ownership of the means of production, then Marxism can save.

We Christians have been misled by our own arrogance. At times we have thought that to affirm Christ as *the* way to salvation meant that everything good or virtuous came only through Christ. This was wrong. But in recognizing this error and realizing that certain virtues outside Christianity match or excel those inside, Christians today are tempted to make the same mistake in reverse and assume that all kinds of salvation are present in all forms of faith. This is the flip side of the same arrogance.

The Christian claim is in one sense a narrow one. It is that Christ is the sole and decisive mediator of one salvation: forgiveness, reconciliation, and restoration to communion with the personal God and creator of us all. Christians obviously think *this* salvation is the most important thing in the world. Whether it is so or not, it is plainly not the only thing in the world. If you think it is an illusion or that something else is more important, you will not bother with it. You will be much more interested in other forms of salvation, and you will find other forms of faith as good or better at providing them.

It is possible that if your burning concern is for moral transformation or historical change, or for that matter if your concern is with the metaphysical basis for a pluralistic society, you may be led toward Christianity by another route. Christianity may begin to seem a live option because of some of the by-products it seems to bring in its wake, rather than because of the conviction that lies at its heart. But we cannot deal with the functional virtues of Christianity (or any faith) without also opening the question of its fundamental truth.

The proper relationship of Christianity to other faiths, then, is one of honest pluralism. The differences are real. One of the fundamental differences between Christianity and Buddhism, for example, has been expressed this way by a Buddhist: "Buddhism declares that there is from the beginning no self to crucify. To think that there is the self is the start of all errors and evils. . . . As there is no self, no crucifixion is needed, no sadism is to be practiced, no shocking sight is to be displayed by the roadside."[7]

The relationship between Christianity and Hinduism, to take another example, poses a contrast between a framework of belief which subordinates the personal to the impersonal and one that does exactly the reverse. To the Hindu it is hopelessly naive to suppose that ultimate reality is itself truly personal, even if we picture it that way. To the Christian it is impossible not to suppose that relationships are of ultimate significance and that the impersonal must be interpreted in terms of the personal. These differences are too sharp and go too deep into the very texture of the way we live our lives to somehow be papered over with talk of "opposites in creative tension." One very prominent writer in this field has said that no one comes to God as personal "Father" except through Christ.

> But millions of men and women may in Buddhism have come to God as release out of suffering into *Nirvana*; or . . . in Hinduism to God as many-sided source and meaning of life . . . And further, it may be that Christ . . . is also present in these other religions, and their several awarenesses of God likewise present [to some extent] in Christianity. . . .[8]

This statement acknowledges the real differences, but immediately insists that what is encountered in every case is the same God. This is the assumption which I think needs to be rejected, at least in such simple form. Why should we suppose that the Buddhist, despite his or her best efforts to the contrary, really gets a personal God? This may sound like a friendly thing to say of Buddhism. From a Christian point of view, it is, but it is more or less the same thing as saying that Buddhism is a failure on its own terms.

There are strong mystical streams in Christianity which at times may produce statements that sound "Hindu," just as there may be a branch of Buddhism which has something like a "savior" figure. Such impressionistic parallels, however, do not go very far toward establishing the idea that all religions contain, to some degree, all the pieces of God. Not all the pieces belong to the same puzzle. However similar in appearance two bits from two religions may be, we have to remember that each stands not alone but within a whole framework of belief. The more you assemble the similar bits from different faiths, the more it becomes clear that they do not fit together in the same way.

It is simple enough, for instance, to study religions comparatively and to note how founders are inevitably deified in some sense, represented in art, raised up in statues. So we see the enormous golden Buddhas of Asia, the great-coated Lenins on every Russian square, the crucifixes. All are undeniably statues. But other things are undeniable also. The Buddha's hands are always open, renouncing all and holding fast to nothing. Lenin's hand is always closed and raised in a fist. Christ's hands are always pierced, neither open nor closed.[9] So it is with the faiths they represent. They are not different in *every* respect—that is hardly conceivable—but the differences are crucial.

Does this mean that the various faiths have nothing to learn from one another? Not at all. Christian theology is clarified in dialogue with other faiths. Islam's perennial questions to Christians about the Trinity, for instance, are helpful in forcing us to explain our commitment to the monotheism which both faiths prize so highly, and in guarding us from the error of distorting the Trinity into polytheism.

In encountering the theological traditions of others, we may be stimulated to recover elements that belong to Christianity but have been lost or marginalized. The stress upon feminine imagery of the divine in some faiths has led Christianity to look at its own Scriptures afresh. In doing so we see not only the condemnations of the fertility cults which surrounded Israel but, all the more striking for being preserved and affirmed in that environment, the feminine images used of God.[10] Even further, there may be certain things—postures and techniques of prayer, for instance—that are not a part of Christian tradition at all but could be profitably integrated into Christian life.

Such learning can clarify our faith, rediscover lost elements, even add new elements compatible with Christian essentials. However, it cannot create what is not there, nor eliminate what is central. Images and art and music and concepts from other cultures and even other faiths can enrich the expression and understanding of the Christian gospel, but we cannot add a once-for-all incarnation of God in Christ to Hinduism and still have Hinduism. We cannot add Buddhist *karma* to the Christian will of God and still have Christianity.

The limits of learning are broad, but there are limits. They are posed by the nature of truth on the one hand, and the identities of the faiths on the other. Individuals can experience conversion from one faith to another and retain their identity. They experience conversion as a way of becoming more truly themselves, however radically they may change their past behavior or beliefs. Faiths themselves cannot convert. They can adapt and develop within certain boundaries, but to transgress those boundaries is to lose their identity.

God or Christ?

Even if Christian faith does hold fast to its basic differences with other faiths, must it necessarily focus these so exclusively on Christ? We have spoken of the sense in which Hinduism and Buddhism, for example, representing different frameworks of ultimate belief, are searching for different things. Perhaps some readers would have liked to point out that this is not true in the same way for all other faiths. Judaism and Islam represent special cases in that they would appear to be indeed seeking the same thing: reconciliation with the same personal God, the God of Abraham, the God of Jesus, the God of Mohammed. Could not Christians, at least with these traditions, focus on the common threads of faith without always focusing on the points of disagreement?

In fact there is a movement within Christian theology itself which strongly suggests that Christians have come dangerously close to an idolatry of Christ.[11] It is said that our dialogue with Jews and Muslims, not to mention many of our own internal difficulties with Jesus' particularity, would be greatly aided if we were more God-centered and less Christ-centered. Christ divides us from them, being the unique object of worship of only one faith, but God unites, being the common object of worship of at least all who believe in a personal God.

After all, from the Christian point of view, Jesus is the Son and Word of *God*, the servant of *God*, the revealer of *God*. By Jesus' own example, doesn't the focus belong on God? God is inclusive; Christ is exclusive. If we get our priorities straight—and surely no one can argue that God is not the top priority—we can accent the inclusiveness. Muslims have great difficulty in believing the Christian claim that we are monotheists. To them it seems that we are polytheists, with two Gods in eternal tension: a wrathful judge and a merciful Christ. If we want to make good on our claim to believe in one God, then we ought to make it clear that Christ does not belong in the place of God.

We can agree that the distinction between Christ and God is necessary. In the New Testament, for instance, we cannot simply exchange the word "God" at random for the word "Christ" and make sense; for example, "Christ so loved the world that he sent God." Christians are in theological danger if they begin to *replace* God with Christ. Yet for Christians, as we illustrated in our survey of Scripture, it is not possible to *separate* God and Christ.

Despite the superficial plausibility of the idea, we cannot say that what we have in common with Jews and Muslims is our faith in God while what divides us is our particular additional belief in Christ. There is not one identical building block, "God," upon which Christians put another block called "Christ," as opposed to the Muslims who put one called "the Koran."

The God in whom we believe is not quite the same as that of the Jew or Muslim, since our God's character is fundamentally defined by a different standard. For Christians, Christ is God's self-characterization, God spelled out in the fullest way through the deepest language: our human existence itself. It has often been observed that the oldest Christian confessions of faith contained only one article: the one about Christ. For the early Christians, theology was "in reality almost exclusively Christology."[12] This did not mean that they had no concern with God, but that they had found one decisive word about God.

Christian focus on Christ is a *way* of being God-centered, not a substitute for being God-centered. You cannot draw a circle unless you can *locate* the center. To say you want God to be at the center, or that you want to know and follow God, does not take you very far unless you have some definitive way of locating or describing this God. This way is precisely what Christians believe Christ is.

In fact, our definition of something must always include some distinction if it is to be of any use to us. Otherwise we have definitions that tell us nothing: God equals God. That is the value of the incarnation: it defines God through what is *not* God, through unlikeness as well as likeness. To say that we ought to be God-centered instead of Christ-centered sounds like a movement from a more parochial and limited perspective to one that is higher and more comprehensive, but this is not really so.

One theologian was heard to say: "Religions are relative. Only God is absolute. I get nervous when people talk about Christianity as the absolute religion." But, if "Only God is absolute" is to mean anything, it must have some reference point. If God is not decisively known anywhere in particular, then this "God" who is absolute is only what I make God to be, acording to my definition. Thus, in fact, it is myself or my group that I make absolute.

There is no doubt that Islam and Judaism are special cases in relation to Christianity. The special relationship stems from the fact that we share certain descriptive material in our understanding of God. Christians share the Hebrew Scriptures. Muslims share with Christians a certain amount of overlap between the New Testament and the Koran: that is, points on which they agree. But even in what is shared we must acknowledge that this is weighted differently and understood in terms of elements which are *not* shared. Still, dialogue and cooperation with these faiths can proceed on a different basis than with others, for dialogue with them can sometimes have the character of shared interpretation of the *same* material. This may occur, for instance, when Jews and Christians meet to study the Hebrew Scriptures together.

Like most close family relationships, these sometimes seem to hold the potential of greater misunderstanding and deeper hurt than those with more distantly related faiths, but the rewards of these relationships are rich indeed in grasping our own identity as Christians. Discussion and dialogue will not be fruitful, however, unless they proceed honestly from the differing understandings of God in each tradition. Christians themselves will not materially advance these relationships or solve the problem of pluralism by changing their own fundamental faith.

Location and Destination

Probably nothing plays a larger role in the ordinary discussion of pluralism than the question of judgment—heaven and hell. The strongest objection to Christ as decisive savior is the picture of millions of persons consigned to eternal pun-

Is Christ the Only Way? † 145

ishment for lack of faith. It does not matter much that other religious traditions generally either include a notion of hell or regard salvation as a serious hope only for a small elite.

Ordinary common sense today is offended by the idea of judgment. This is partly because of the modern tendency to feel it unfair to be judged by any standards but those we individually select, a tendency to reject any objective standards. For whatever reason, traditional images of the final judgment may recall nothing to the modern mind so much as the arrival of prisoners at Auschwitz, where they were herded before an officer who directed some to one side and to life (at least for the present) and others to another side and to extermination. In the final judgment many would say that only the stakes have been escalated, to paradise and eternal flame.

The key to this popular image of what Christians mean by judgment can be found in a single point. It assumes that people are meted out their fate or condemned *against their wills*. The saints look down from heaven in glee upon tormented souls who are caged and fenced from that bliss they long to share, but bliss will never be theirs, because they failed to believe in Jesus. According to this warped interpretation, people have been rounded up and imprisoned, and will pay an eternal price, with no parole and no time off for good behavior. Our society gives even murderers a second chance, and shows mercy within the space of a mere lifetime, but God, it is said, throws away the key for all eternity.

At this crucial point the popular image could hardly be further off the mark. The point of judgment is not some arbitrary cutoff. Judgment is inseparable from the notion of a "new heaven and new earth." The transformation which is begun "in Christ" is the means to this new reality. Those who do not participate in it are not just in neutral. They continue to be transformed in other ways. It is not that God will not give people a second chance, or a third or a fourth. The simple fact is that we can reach a point where a thousand chances would not make any difference. If they would, they would be given.

This is the truly terrible possibility. We can see it in Jesus' parable of the rich man and Lazarus, where from the anguish of Hades the rich man still speaks of Lazarus as a servant, desiring God to have Lazarus come and serve him. For one who has turned away from God, communion with God is ruled out: notice in the parable that the rich man shows no desire to go where God and Lazarus are, only to have Lazarus come and serve him where he is (Luke 16:19-31).

The Christian gospel implies that no sinful act is irreversible in the sense that it absolutely bars one from salvation, but preference for something other than God can become irreversible. This is, properly speaking, "self-judgment" as we described it in Jesus' ministry and in the New Testament view of Christ as the judge.

I already have said that the Buddhist, for example, is not seeking communion with a personal God and an eternal personal existence. She or he is seeking *nirvana*. Some Marxists and all nonreligious humanists do not seek either of these things, but rather a part in making a new world and a contribution to human posterity. Let us suppose that all succeed.

We should suppose that, in gaining what you want, there is no ground for complaint. To a Christian, the Buddhist *nirvana*, or the Hindu release from reincarnation into the oneness of the raindrop with the sea, or the humanist's legacy to future generations of an ambiguous series of acts "for their good" is not noticeably different from hell. In all of these there is separation from the personal God known in Jesus, the extinction of personal and bodily existence, the end of all relationship.

The story is told of a Unitarian and a Calvinist who were arguing theology. At the conclusion of their discussion the Unitarian said, "Sir, I perceive we are in perfect agreement, with one small reservation: the being which you call your God, I call my devil." In a similar way one might say what the Buddhist calls release, the Christian calls damnation. What the Christian calls heaven, the Buddhist calls ignorance and illusion.

The terrible judgment of God is quite simply this: God will let us have what we really want—if we really want it. Obviously there is nothing terrible about this in principle. It is only our wanting that makes it so.

Dante's *Divine Comedy* provides a classic exposition of what most would regard as the traditional view of hell. As Dante comes to the gates of hell, he reads the inscription above them: "Justice moved my great maker; God eternal wrought me; The power, and the unsearchably high wisdom, and the primal love supernal."[13] Is this to say that hell's foundations were laid in *love*? If we suppose that the highest form of love and respect is to grant freedom and independence to other persons, when we could dominate and coerce them, then logically we must say that hell, as the possibility of going our own way to the very end, is one of the fullest signs of God's love.

In the circles or levels of hell, Dante encounters many persons. They are not chained, or if they are, the chains are of their own making. The punishment they endure is simply "the sin itself, experienced without illusion. . . ."[14] Even to call it "sin," of course, is to speak from a Christian perspective. To the persons there it is not sin. If they truly and completely believed it were so, they would not be where they are. They are there because there they get, all things considered, what they want above everything else.

No one in Dante's hell is totally satisfied there. But no one is totally *unsatisfied* even in the lowest depths. It is in a strange sense heaven for them: the sense in which heaven is our heart's desire. Those in Dante's hell continue to regard heaven itself the same way they regarded it in life. It is not as though the scales have fallen from their eyes and suddenly they see what they have missed. The integrity of their faiths in this sense is maintained eternally.

Life is not a game or a show, a kind of performance where God keeps the prizes under wraps and then, like the conclusion of a detective story, reveals what has really been going on. The options that are before us now remain live options eternally. In other words, the Buddhist is free to remain a Buddhist to the very eternal bliss of *nirvana*. We are free to cling to lesser goods than God, with the attendant hurt that goes with lesser goods, even if that lesser good is extinction.

Of course the Christian believes that these are in truth objectively lesser goods, and that the Christian perspective on these different choices is the valid one. Heaven is objectively real, as communion with God, and it is objectively the true end of humanity, since we are created by God.

But observe the symmetry of this confession with the Buddhist conviction, for instance. That the Christian "goes to heaven" can only mean from the Buddhist point of view that the Christian remains on the path of illusion and bondage to the self. Of course heaven is not "objectively real" to the Buddhist, since the self itself is not so. So the Christian belief that it *is* real is hardly offensive to the Buddhist, but only to be pitied.

God allows, and has even established, what we might call ultimate pluralism, the eternal right of choice and interpretation. No one is compelled to give up her or his view of reality. Yet reality is not "what you make it," though *your* reality can be in large measure what you finally choose it to be.

Someone may say at this point that this may all be true, but, if it is objectively better to be with God, this situation is still unfair. Because of their place of birth, their culture, and so on, people do not start even in terms of what they want. They are, in a sense, predetermined to follow one way to the end as opposed to another. Here we need to come back to what was said earlier about the fact that God *is* present everywhere and also about the fact that each religious tradition does have various streams and elements within it.

Those who truly desire God—and this desire may arise slowly, require long separation from other desires—will be led by the Holy Spirit toward closer communion with God. This may happen completely within a religious tradition other than Christianity. Within a religious tradition that is not theistic, there are tendencies that move toward a knowledge of God's existence, and perhaps further toward the personal character of God. Within those that attribute no moral significance to ultimate reality, there are streams that move in this direction. Even within those that regard the historical and the particular as unimportant and inferior compared to the cyclical and the eternal, there are some groups that show support for the opposite view. Not all of Christian faith lies hidden in other faiths, but within other traditions one can move *toward rather than away from* what Christians believe to be the truth.

This movement is not necessarily complete or decisive with

death. If the search is to be fully satisfied, however, it must come finally to Christ, or walk *with* Christ. The other side of the picture is that even those who live and die within *nominal* Christianity may be moving constantly toward another end, seeking something other than the personal God of Christ. In our fellowship with people of other faiths we can then say and believe that we *may* be on the path to the same destination, if we understand the open-endedness of that statement: they may finally come to Christ, or we may finally *not*! Here the special care and warnings about judgment which Christ gave only to his disciples and not to those outside are much to the point.

The moment of death is then not completely decisive. The trajectory on which we leave this life is desperately important, however. The possibility of conversion—in either direction—is not ended with death. But as our desires and wants become fixed, they more and more approach a "point of no return." At that point, though we remain free to choose as we please, we cannot please as we please. What we want is decided, and no matter how often or constantly God's grace is offered to us to help us want something else, it is of no avail. We have consummated our freedom by transforming ourselves. The freedom that is given to us in the image of God is real, including the freedom to make irrevocable choices.

Pluralism, far from being a mere phase of history or a surface appearance, is in principle a possibility which God leaves open to us even ultimately. There is, in theory, no limit to God's willingness to uphold our freedom and to respect our choices. But we have no way and no need to know whether these plural possibilities, which God "holds open" for us, will in fact be eternally realized.

We should not forget to note also the role of justice in the biblical vision of judgment. Those who served Christ, who sought the reign of God as they journeyed toward Christ, and who were cut off—the martyrs, the innocents, the "disappeared" of our own age—these reach that for which they aim, that for which they were remaking themselves. They are vindicated in pure justice, at no one else's expense. By the same token, those for whom lesser goods and small evils, and finally great evils, had become meat and drink, have that for which they made themselves.

From this point of view, both evangelism and dialogue with other faiths are crucially important. The first is crucially important because right now *is* always a decisive time for persons who are making their way toward or away from the God of Christ. Dialogue, too, is important not only for understanding and cooperation, but also because other faith traditions are full of persons who are in truth on their way to the God who was in Christ. Our present location does not decree our destination.

We can never know infallibly what that means within another tradition. Nevertheless, the better we know those faiths from the inside, the better we will sense where in a deep sense we can affirm them and where in our dialogue we must speak critically, as we are willing to listen. We must be very sensitive to their understandings of us, for they will teach us where we, within the supposed security of *the* way and truth and life, are in fact moving away from the very God we confess and proclaim.

This dialogue and relationship ought to proceed with respect and without animosity, since we pose no threat to each other. We are not competitors for the same thing. We are seekers after various things, and what those things are will not always in truth correspond to the labels we wear.

Evangelism and dialogue are two different processes. Nevertheless, dialogue will teach us how to be honest and honorable evangelists. This is a crucial part of being successful evangelists, since as Christians we must define success not only by numbers but also by faithfulness to Christ in our methods and effect. Dialogue, when it embodies both honesty and trust, will reach points where the only full way to dialogue is to *confess*, each from his or her own ground, what animates us and fills us.

For Christians this will mean, now and always, to confess Christ, Christ in particular, on a cross, alive from a tomb, reigning in grace, for the life of the world.

•

Suggestions for Further Reading

Aldwinckle, Russell, *Jesus: A Savior or the Savior?* Macon, Ga.: Mercer University Press, 1982.

Hick, John, *God Has Many Names.* Philadelphia: The Westminster Press, 1982.

Neill, Stephen, *Christian Faith and Other Faiths.* New York: Oxford University Press, 1970.

Newbigin, Lesslie, *The Finality of Christ.* Richmond: John Knox Press, 1969.

Robinson, J.A.T., *Truth Is Two-Eyed.* Philadelphia: The Westminster Press, 1980.

Samartha, S.J., ed., *Faith in the Midst of Faiths.* Geneva: World Council of Churches, 1977.

Notes

Chapter 1

[1] In the discussion that follows I am indebted to insights from Lesslie Newbigin's *The Finality of Christ* (Richmond: John Knox Press, 1969), pp. 11-15.

[2] An exquisite brief treatment of this "game" and its rules is C.S. Lewis's essay "Bulverism" in *God in the Dock* (Grand Rapids: William B. Eerdmans Publishing Co., 1970), pp. 271-277.

[3] See John Hick, ed., *The Myth of God Incarnate* (Philadelphia: The Westminster Press, 1978).

[4] See Leslie G. Howard, *The Expansion of God* (Maryknoll, N.Y.: Orbis Books, 1981), p. 338.

[5] As an illustration of this religious sensibility, see the vision of the goddess described at the end of Apuleius's *The Golden Ass*, trans. Jack Lindsay (Bloomington: Indiana University Press, 1960), pp. 237-238. The goddess describes herself as the "uniform manifestation of all the gods and goddesses" and as the "single godhead venerated all over the earth under manifold forms, varying rites and changing names."

Chapter 2

[1] Stephen Neill, *A History of Christian Missions* (New York: Penguin Books, 1964), p. 323. See also p. 262.

[2] Jane and James Ritchie, *Growing Up in Polynesia* (London: Allen & Unwin, 1979). Also see John Garrett, *To Live Among the Stars* (Geneva: World Council of Churches, 1982).

[3] Dr. Singh's full address has been distributed as one of the documents of the Sixth Assembly of the World Council of Churches: "Address by Dr. Gopal

Singh on behalf of guests from the non-Christian faiths to the World Assembly at Vancouver," document AD-7.

⁴ See Kenneth S. Kantzer, "Revitalizing World Evangelism: The Lausanne Congress Ten Years Later," *Christianity Today*, June 15, 1984, p. 10.

Chapter 3

¹ For a brief introduction to the discussion, see William R. Farmer, "The Dynamic of Christianity: The Question of Development between Jesus and Paul," *Religion in Life*, 38 (1969), pp. 570-577.

² See James D. G. Dunn, *Christology in the Making* (Philadelphia: The Westminster Press, 1980), p. 252, and the material elsewhere in the book which leads to this conclusion.

³ For an excellent exposition and defense of this view, see C.F.D. Moule, *The Origin of Christology* (Cambridge: Cambridge University Press, 1977).

⁴ See Mary Daly, *Beyond God the Father* (Boston: Beacon Press, 1973), pp. 69-97.

⁵ See James H. Cone, *Black Theology and Black Power* (New York: The Seabury Press, 1969), p. 32, and *God of the Oppressed* (New York: The Seabury Press, 1975), pp. 33f.

⁶ See, for instance, the various stages in the development of the Nicene Creed as given in Henry Bettenson, ed., *Documents of the Christian Church* (New York: Oxford University Press, 1947), pp. 35-37. The word *sarkothena* ("was made flesh") emphasizes common humanity and the word *enanthropesanta* ("and became human") explicitly uses the generic *anthropos* to mean human, rather than the ready alternative *aner* to mean a male.

Chapter 4

¹ For an excellent survey of present scholarship in this vein, see R.H. Fuller and Pheme Perkins, *Who Is This Christ?* (Philadelphia: Fortress Press, 1983).

² Dietrich Bonhoeffer, *The Cost of Discipleship*, trans. R.H. Fuller (London: SCM Press, 1959), p. 79.

³ See Acts 10:38, John 1:32, and Luke 9:35.

⁴ The translation is by C.H. Dodd. See J.A.T. Robinson, *The Human Face of God* (Philadelphia: The Westminster Press, 1979), p. 188.

⁵ See James D.G. Dunn, *Christology in the Making* (Philadelphia: The Westminster Press, 1980), especially pp. 210ff. and 262ff.

⁶ Jesus says "my father" 17 times in Matthew, 4 times in Luke, and 25 times in John. The expressions "their father" or "your father" occur some 19 times.

⁷ Ernst Fuchs, *Studies of the Historical Jesus*, trans. Andrew Scobie (Naperville, Ill.: Alec R. Allenson, Inc., 1964), p. 22.

⁸ The same essential point, without the claim to be the *chief* of sinners, can be made from many passages in the generally accepted Pauline letters, as in Galatians 1:4, 2:17.

⁹ On this point see Oscar Cullmann, *The Christology of the New Testament*, trans. S.C. Guthrie and C.A.M. Hall (Philadelphia: The Westminster Press, 1980), especially pp. 51-82.

Chapter 5

¹ C.F.D. Moule makes this point in his chapter "The Scope of the Death of Christ," in *Origin of Christology* (Cambridge: Cambridge University Press, 1977). This paragraph and the next draw upon some of the points made in that chapter.

² For a good compendium of the biblical material, assembled with this

Notes † 155

question in mind, see Ronald Sider, ed., *Cry Justice* (New York: Paulist Press, 1980).

³On this, see Reinhold Niebuhr, *The Nature and Destiny of Man* (New York: Charles Scribner's Sons, 1964), Volume I, especially chapters seven and eight. Niebuhr explicates the two sides of sin, which he calls pride and sensuality. His schematic approach is basically sound, but my own description of what he calls "sensuality" is somewhat different from his and reflects what I believe to be the valid criticism of such feminist theologians as Valerie Saiving.

⁴Lady Helen Oppenheimer, *Incarnation and Immanence* (London: Hodder and Stoughton, 1973), pp. 17f.

⁵1 Corinthians 12:12-13; Romans 12:5; Galatians 3:27.

⁶See also 1 Corinthians 15:27 and Ephesians 1:22. C.H. Dodd has argued that the varied use of this psalm in the New Testament points to a well-established tradition in the early church. See his *According to the Scriptures* (New York: Charles Scribner's Sons, 1953), pp. 32-34. Also see F.F. Bruce, *The Epistle to the Hebrews* (London: Marshall, Morgan & Scott, 1964), pp. 32-37.

⁷Paul M. van Buren, *The Secular Meaning of the Gospel* (New York: Macmillan Publishing Co., 1966), p. 54.

⁸This paragraph draws upon J.D.G. Dunn, *Jesus and the Spirit* (Philadelphia: The Westminster Press, 1975), pp. 194f.

⁹The substance of this saying of Jesus has very strong support in the Gospel sources: Mark 9:37; Matthew 18:5; Luke 9:48; Matthew 10:40; Luke 10:16; and John 13:20. J.A.T. Robinson discusses this in *The Human Face of God* (Philadelphia: The Westminster Press, 1979), p. 214.

¹⁰See Romans 5:12-21; 1 Corinthians 15:22; and 1 Corinthians 15:45-47.

¹¹Madeleine L'Engle, *The Irrational Season* (New York: The Seabury Press, 1977), pp. 111-112.

¹²The quotation is from the Revised Standard Version with the exception that the word *anthropois*—a word which refers to generic humanity—is given with a non-sex-specific equivalent.

Chapter 7

¹The substance of the typology which I use in this chapter comes from my colleague Gabriel Fackre. See "The Scandals of Particularity and Universality," *Mid-Stream*, 22 (January 1983), pp. 32-52.

²See Krister Stendahl, "Notes for Three Biblical Studies," in Gerald Anderson and Thomas Stransky, eds., *Christ's Lordship and Religious Pluralism* (Maryknoll, N.Y.: Orbis Books, 1981), pp. 13-15.

³Perhaps the most influential statement of the view that Christianity is the absolute religion for Western humanity is Ernst Troeltsch's *The Absoluteness of Christianity and the History of Religions*, trans. David Reid (Richmond: John Knox Press, 1971).

⁴John Hick is one of the most prominent exponents of such a global theology. See *God and the Universe of Faiths,*. revised edition (Philadelphia: The Westminster Press, 1982) and *God Has Many Names* (Philadelphia: The Westminster Press, 1982).

⁵This view is characteristic of Wilfred Cantwell Smith, *Towards a World Theology* (Philadelphia: The Westminster Press, 1981).

⁶The "scripture" of the Unification Church, *Divine Principle*, presents itself as a synthesis of the religious wisdom of East and West. The Unification Church, however, as is most often the case, does not simply proclaim an assimilation of different religious truths, but claims to bring them together

through the medium of a further, and truly final revelation. In this sense it is like Mormonism.

⁷Schubert M. Ogden, *The Reality of God* (London: SCM Press, 1967), p. 173.

⁸Many may remember diagrams in secondary school science texts which illustrated the way in which the molecules in a piece of metal line up when magnetized. Without this restructuring the random character of the molecules' arrangement prevents them from exercising any electromagnetic power.

⁹This is a phrase which has become particularly associated with the Roman Catholic theologian Karl Rahner. Indeed the view described in this section approximates Rahner's position. See Karl Rahner, *Foundations of Christian Faith*, trans. William V. Dych (New York: Crossroad Publishing Co., 1982), pp. 138-321.

¹⁰See Raimundo Panikkar, *The Unknown Christ of Hinduism* (Maryknoll, N.Y.: Orbis Books, 1981).

¹¹This option is in many ways associated with the position adopted by Karl Barth. See his *Church Dogmatics*, trans. G.W. Bromiley (Edinburgh: T. and T. Clark, 1956, 1958, 1961, 1962), Volume IV, Parts 1, 2, 3a, 3b.

¹²Sir Norman Anderson, *Christianity and Comparative Religion* (London: Tyndale House, 1970), p. 104.

Chapter 8

¹John Hick, ed. *The Myth of God Incarnate* (Philadelphia: The Westminster Press, 1978), p. 181.

²A. Michael Ramsey, *God, Christ and the World* (London: SCM Press, 1969), p. 68.

³Quoted in H.R. Mackintosh, *The Doctrine of the Person of Christ* (Edinburgh: T. and T. Clark, 1962), p. 231.

⁴Lesslie Newbigin, *op. cit.*, p. 115.

⁵This summary comes from "Christ and Christianity," in *The Finality of Christ*, ed. Dow Kirkpatrick (Nashville: Abingdon Press, 1966), p. 198.

⁶I have been helped by Gabriel Fackre's formulation of this point. See his "The Scandals of Particularity and Universality," *Mid-Stream*, 22 (January 1983), pp. 32-52.

⁷D.T. Suzuki, *Mysticism, Christian and Buddhist* (New York: Harper & Row, Publishers, Inc., 1957), pp. 136-137.

⁸John Hick, "The Reconstruction of Christian Belief," *Theology*, 73 (September, 1970), pp. 404f.

⁹Kosuke Koyama, *No Handle on the Cross* (Maryknoll, N.Y.: Orbis Books, 1977), pp. 22-27.

¹⁰See for example Phyllis Trible, *God and the Rhetoric of Sexuality* (Philadelphia: Fortress Press, 1978).

¹¹See Jean Milet, *God or Christ?* (New York: Crossroad Publishing Co., 1981).

¹²See Oscar Cullmann, *Christology of the New Testament*, trans. S.C. Guthrie and C.A.M. Hall (Philadelphia: The Westminster Press, 1980), pp. 2-3. Some examples of early Christian confessions would be 1 Corinthians 8:6; John 1:3; Colossians 1:16; Hebrews 1:10.

¹³Dante Alighieri, *The Divine Comedy: Hell*, trans. Dorothy Sayers (New York: Penguin Books, 1973), p. 85.

¹⁴*Ibid.*, p. 102.

Index

Abba (father), 74, 82, 90
Anderson, Sir Norman, 156 (chapter 7, n.12)
Animism, 17
Anonymous Christianity, 121, 124, 137
Apuleius, 153 (chapter 1, n.5)
Auschwitz, 145
Avatar, 24

Bach, Johann Sebastian, 69
Bad conscience, 18, 20
Bahái, 46, 116
Barth, Karl, 156 (chapter 7, n.11)
Bettenson, Henry, p. 154 (chapter 3, n.6)
Bible, 17, 56-59, 69, 92, 107, 112, 133, 141
Body of Christ, 89
Bonhoeffer, Dietrich, 70, 154 (chapter 4, n.2)
Bronson, Miles, 44-45
Bruce, F.F., 155 (chapter 5, n.6)
Buddhism, 17, 36-37, 114, 116, 121, 138-141, 146-148

Carey, William, 40

Christ, see Jesus Christ
Colonialism, 19, 40-42
Cone, James H., 154 (chapter 3, n.5)
Confucianism, 17
Conversion, 46-50, 56, 126, 141, 149
Creation, 107, 125-126
Crucifixion, 80-81
Cullmann, Oscar, 154 (chapter 4, n.9), 156 (chapter 8, n.12)
Cultural imperialism, 42-45

Daly, Mary, 154 (chapter 3, n.4)
Dante Alighieri, 146-147, 156 (chapter 8, n.13)
Dialogue, 117, 144, 150
Dodd, C.H., 154 (chapter 4, n.4), 155 (chapter 5, n.6)
Dunn, James D.G., 154 (chapter 3, n.2), 155 (chapter 5, n.8)

East, 19, 37, 115
Eschatology, 95-100, 102, 144-147
Evangelism, 20, 22, 47-48, 112, 118, 125-126, 150
Evolution, 53

Fackre, Gabriel, 155 (chapter 7, n.1), 156 (chapter 8, n.6)
Faiths, 17, 22, 30-31, 48, 112-116, 124, 132, 137-142
Farmer, William R., 154 (chapter 3, n.1)
Feminism, 60-63, 87
Forgiveness, 75-78, 130
Freud, Sigmund, 21
Fuchs, Ernst, 154 (chapter 4, n.7)
Fuller, R. H., 154 (chapter 4, n.1)

Gandhi, Mahatma, 116
Garrett, John, 153 (chapter 2, n.2)
Global theology, 115-117

Heaven, 144-147
Hell, 144-147
Hick, John, 153 (chapter 1, n.3), 155 (chapter 7, n.4), 156 (chapter 8, n.1,8)
Hinduism, 17, 36-37, 113-115, 121, 136-141, 146
Hiroshima, 38
History, 16-17, 106-108
Holocaust, 38
Holy Spirit, 73-74, 100, 126-127, 148
Hope, 136
Howard, Leslie G., 153 (chapter 1, n.4)
Human nature, 65-66, 85, 87
Human rights, 65-66
Humanism, 17, 146

Idolatry, 38, 142
Incarnation, 24-25, 69-70, 143
India, 24, 41
Innocence, 77
Islam, 17, 20, 36, 48, 58, 114-115, 121, 136-137, 141-144
Israel, 71, 79, 101, 103, 106, 107

Jesus Christ, 16, 23-26, 114, 116, 118-122; objections to, 51-66; particularity of, 54-66; relation to God, 69-75; and forgiveness, 75-78; death of, 73, 78-85; inclusive person, 88-94; divinity, 63-64, 69, 92; and judgment, 78-79, 97, 99-103; and history, 106-108; the way, 129-131; the truth, 131-134; the life, 134-137; God or, 142-144

Jews (and Judaism), 25, 34-38, 72, 101-104, 114-115, 142-144
Judgment, 78-79, 95-103, 145-146
Justice, 95-99, 127, 135-137, 149

Kantzer, Kenneth, 154 (chapter 2, n.4)
Kirkpatrick, Dow, 156 (chapter 8, n.5)
Knowledge of God, 103-104, 113, 118, 121, 132
Koran, 58, 144
Koyama, Kosuke, 156 (chapter 8, n.9)

Language, 112
L'Engle, Madeleine, 155 (chapter 5, n.11)
Lenin, 140-141
Lewis, C. S., 153 (chapter 1, n.2)
Love, 14-15
Luther, Martin, 131

Mackintosh, H.R., 156 (chapter 8, n.3)
Marxism, 17, 48, 87, 138, 146
Merton, Thomas, 116
Milet, Jean, 156 (chapter 8, n.11)
Missionaries, 38-42, 57
Morality, 14-15, 26, 65, 78, 105-106
Moule, C.F.D., 154 (chapter 3, n.3 and chapter 5, n.1)

Neibuhr, Reinhold, 155 (chapter 5, n.3)
Neill, Stephen, 153 (chapter 2, n.1)
Newbigin, Lesslie, 153 (chapter 1, n.1), 156 (chapter 8, n.4)
Nishga, 45
Nuclear threat, 49

Ogden, Schubert M., 156 (chapter 7, n.7)
Oppenheimer, Lady Helen, 155 (chapter 5, n.4)

Pacific Islands, 41, 43, 59
Panikkar, Raimundo, 156 (chapter 7, n.10)
Particularity, 51-56, 63-66; magnetic particularity, 120-122; healing particularity, 122-125; imperial particularity, 125-127

Paul, 51-52, 54, 74, 84, 89, 91, 93, 101, 104, 106
Perkins, Pheme, 154 (chapter 4, n.1)
Pluralism, 29-31, 34-38, 48-49, 64, 135, 139-140, 148; parallel pluralism, 111-114; picture puzzle pluralism, 114-117; degree pluralism, 117-120
Prejudice, 27-28
Presuppositions, 13-14
Prophets, 71-72, 81, 97
Protestantism, 123
Psychoanalysis, 87
Puritans, 136

Racism, 18-19, 60-62
Rahner, Karl, 156 (chapter 7, n.9)
Ramsey, A. Michael, 156 (chapter 8, n.2)
Religion, 17-18, 26-27, 30-31, 46, 117-119, 138
Representation, 71-74, 79-80, 84-94, 101, 105, 107, 131
Resurrection, 64, 84, 90, 92-93, 102
Revelation, 103, 119, 134
Richie, Jane and James, 153 (chapter 2, n.2)
Robinson, J. A. T., 154 (chapter 4, n.4), 155 (chapter 5, n.9)
Roman Catholicism, 121, 123, 127

Saiving, Valerie, 155 (chapter 5, n.3)
Salvation, 85-88, 92, 97, 101-103, 112-114, 116, 118, 120-122, 124, 126-127, 131, 135, 137-139

Sayers, Dorothy, 156 (chapter 8, n.13, 14)
Science, 16, 87, 133
Sexism, 59-62
Shintoism, 138
Sider, Ron, 154 (chapter 5, n.2)
Sin, 19-20, 75, 77-78, 80-81, 85-88, 91, 101, 105, 123, 125, 130, 134-135, 147
Singh, Gopal, 41, 153 (chapter 2, n.3)
Smith, Wilfred Cantwell, 155 (chapter 7, n.5)
Stendahl, Krister, 155 (chapter 7, n.2)
Suffering servant, 80
Suzuki, D.T., 156 (chapter 8, n.7)

Technology, 18-19, 44-45
Trible, Phyllis, 156 (chapter 8, n.10)
Trinity, 64, 141
Troeltsch, Ernst, 155 (chapter 7, n.3)
Truth, 14-18, 21-22, 27-28, 31, 35-38, 49, 56, 63, 113, 115-117, 131-134

Unification Church, 116, 155 (chapter 7, n.6)

van Buren, Paul M., 155 (chapter 5, n.7)
Vindication, 98

West, 18-20, 36, 39-40, 42-44, 55
Women, 59-63